The OCD Travel Guide

Finding Your Way in a World Full of Risk, Discomfort, and Uncertainty

Michael Parker, LCSW

The Center for OCD and Anxiety Press

ISBN- 978-1-7364091-3-8

Cover design by Michael Parker

Library of Congress Control Number: 2020925797

Printed in the United States of America

The author and publisher have made all efforts to ensure that this book provides an accurate and complete introduction to OCD and its treatment at press time. However, neither the author nor the publisher is engaged in providing specific advice or services to the individual reader. The ideas and suggestions contained in this book are not intended as a substitute for advice from a medical professional. The reader should consult a physician in all health-related matters, particularly with respect to any symptoms that may require diagnosis or medical attention. Neither the author nor the publisher shall be liable or responsible for any loss, damage or disruption allegedly arising from any information or suggestion in this book.

To Milan and Yohan for boundless joy

To Sapna for being my constant

To Mom and Dad for making all things possible

Contents

Selected handouts and worksheets from this book are available for download at:

https://pittsburghocdtreatment.com/publications/the-ocd-travel-guide/

Preface

If you're reading this book, chances are you at least suspect you have Obsessive Compulsive Disorder. And if so, like so many others with OCD, you are looking for help in dealing with it. Because, let's face it, having OCD can be pretty rough. Everyday tasks that come easy to others can be an exhausting battle for you. Your average day is turbulent, uncomfortable, stressful, and draining. Dark and disturbing concerns, to which others seem oblivious, are on your mind from morning until night. And many of the things you want for yourself feel out of reach. But having a full and rich life is totally possible. Living with OCD simply requires a different set of rules. And you're not going to find these rules in most places, because they run counterintuitive to everything you've been taught about happiness in the modern world. This travel guide is going to show you how to map out a life for yourself as someone living with OCD. It's not going to look like everyone else's path in life. And that's okay. Because as someone who has learned how to live with OCD, you're going to be a guru on how to maintain a healthy relationship with your brain. And you're going to have made peace with some of the harsher realities of life: things like uncertainty, risk and discomfort. And you'll have survived more adversity than most will ever know. And if you can manage all of that, you're going to be able to handle anything else life throws at you. So safe travels, and let's get started!

Michael Parker, LCSW

Introduction

Meet Your Annoying, but Inseparable, Travel Companion (aka. OCD)

Living with OCD can sometimes feel like you've been stuck with an unwanted travel companion on your life's journey. You never asked for this companion, but no matter how hard you try, you just can't seem to shake it. And OCD can be the worst sort of partner you could ask for. It's an incessant back seat driver that makes you doubt your every move. Its directions constantly lead you off course from where you were intending to go. It sees everything as too risky, and usually convinces you of all the reasons not to do the super fun thing that everyone else is doing. But OCD is also a charmer, and despite its bad advice, it convinces you to listen. It can make you believe that a low probability concern like botulism is the most imminent threat to your daily well-being. It can make you doubt anything: your goodness, your intentions, your own memory. It can even make a flat-out falsehood like "You are an incompetent person" seem like the essential truth of your life. And it can get you to agree to organize your entire life around these concerns.

And yet OCD isn't getting up to leave anytime soon. In many ways, your OCD is a part of who you are. So don't expect to hear any talk of "curing" or "annihilating" or "wiping out" OCD in this book (that's simply not possible and might not be all that desirable anyway). What this book is going to do is provide you with guidance on how to manage your OCD and greatly reduce your symptoms. You're going to stop all of that overthinking and learn to trust yourself again, and you're going to gain the confidence you need to get back to doing things again. In short, you're going to learn how you can take back control of your life, even with OCD tagging along.

One Diagnosis, Many Stories

It's important to recognize that the story of how, and when, OCD first came into your life is a story unique to you. And the same goes for the nature

1

of the relationship you've developed with your OCD over the years. Maybe you hate your OCD. Maybe you sort of like it. Maybe you're not sure what to think. To highlight just how varied the OCD experience can be, let's look at some stories from others who are also making this journey through life with OCD.

Zach and "The Lifelong Friend"

Zach started to experience OCD at a very young age. Before he was even old enough to go to school, he began to worry about dangerous things like electrical wires and other people's dogs. He would experience images of bloody dog bites and hospital rooms with doctors sticking him with needles, and he tried to avoid activities that could lead to these scenarios. Initially, he didn't see these OCD symptoms as a problem. In fact, he was happy to be aware of these dangers, so that he could avoid situations that posed potential dangers. He learned to never go anywhere near any power cables or electronic devices, and how to scream and cry whenever he was near a dog (this always seemed to cause his Mom to immediately remove him from the situation). But it wasn't until a health class on germs in 5th grade when Zach learned just how helpful OCD could be. The teacher taught everyone about the microscopic bugs that were crawling over everything and yet invisible to the naked eye. Almost immediately after this class, Zach began to experience intrusive "what if" thoughts about the potentially dangerous germs that could exist on the surfaces that he touched, and in the air that he breathed. Zach began washing his hands multiple times an hour with scalding hot water. He altogether stopped touching his face with his hands. He tried his best to keep his distance from others and whenever he did have to interact with someone, he took care to only breath in air when they had stopped speaking, which was particularly stressful and difficult during the extensive lectures from his parents about his handwashing. Overall, though, things seemed to go pretty well through most of elementary and middle school. Zach didn't end up getting sick too often and, as long as he completed all of his avoidant behaviors, he could keep his fear and anxiety under control. It wasn't until high school when Zach first began to wonder if OCD was always being a

2

helpful friend. He tired of having hands that were perpetually red, dry, and cracked. He didn't have as many friends as he would have liked, since he was always trying to avoid others, and their breath, as much as possible. And his peers seemed to be having ideas about where they wanted to go in life. Teachers were beginning to ask about college and career and Zach felt like he didn't have much to say. All he knew was that he didn't want to get sick. He wasn't sure of much else beyond that. After years and years of seeing his cautious nature as a positive, Zach began to wonder what it would be like to not have to think about germs all the time. One fateful night in 11th grade, when Zach accidentally touched the dirty laundry and, without washing his hands, took a bite of food, he had a complete and utter meltdown. After a dramatic and emotional few hours, far past everyone's bedtime, Zach and his parents decided it was time to finally find the right treatment and help Zach manage his OCD.

Kai and "The Sometimes Companion"

OCD came in and out of Kai's life on several occasions. Her first bout came on a particularly difficult day when she had been feeling stressed about school and friends. In the middle of a math class, she felt a strange sensation in her stomach, and asked to go to the bathroom. In a state of anxiety, and crouched over the toilet for 20 minutes, she proceeded to throw up (or at least she thought she threw up. Something definitely came out of her mouth. She thinks). In the months that followed, OCD made her intensely fearful that she could throw up again. Every sensation in her body seemed another sign that she might be on the verge of throwing up. And she began to do all that she could to prevent that from happening. She tried to stay away from anyone who "looked" sick. She avoided the foods she had eaten on the day she threw up (eggs, a granola bar, mac n' cheese, and potato chips). She even made sure not to wear the clothes she had worn that day. And just in case the awful thing came true, and she did have to throw up again, she made sure to always have a path plotted in her mind to the nearest bathroom. When things worsened to the point of Kai starting to miss a few days of school every week, her parents discussed the situation with Kai's pediatrician, and

3

she was prescribed medication for anxiety. This, in conjunction with some visits to the school counselor seemed to do the trick. And after a few months, OCD just seemed to leave as quickly as it came. For good, Kai had hoped.

But OCD had different plans. At the start of Kai's senior year, with college applications right around the corner, OCD dropped right back into her life. She suddenly found herself plagued with fears that she might have cancer. Every bump she noticed on her body triggered a thought that she could have a malignant tumor growing beneath her skin. And she soon found herself spending hours each day trying to figure out if her lymph nodes were swollen, and if that might mean she had thyroid cancer. Kai started to spend hours examining her body and researching cancer symptoms online. And she couldn't figure out how to stop worrying that she was dying. Kai eventually started treatment at an Intensive Outpatient Program, and once she was able to adjust her medication and learn new skills in therapy, she managed to push OCD out of her life once again. By the time she graduated, she was barely worrying about cancer at all.

For a long while, Kai felt free. She finished college, went on to complete graduate school in elementary education, and landed a job she absolutely loved as a 3rd grade teacher. She married a man she adored and became pregnant with their first child. And then it happened again. After the birth of her baby girl, OCD came back with a vengeance. Almost overnight, Kai was worrying about every mark on her baby's skin, every bump and protrusion she didn't think she'd ever noticed before, every cough that came from her little girl's mouth. OCD had her spending all day thinking about cancer and pneumonia and scoliosis and flu. It tortured her with disturbing images of her sweet, little baby girl in the hospital, on a ventilator, even images of her dying. Kai felt despondent. She didn't understand why she was suffering again, and worse than ever before. She talked to her doctor about getting OCD treatment. She was connected with a local OCD therapist and a psychiatrist who could reassess her meds. As she readied herself for a return to treatment, she wondered if she was destined to have OCD pulling this disappearing and reappearing act for the rest of her life.

Jaya and "The Bully"

Jaya started to worry that she was a bad person sometime around middle school. That's when she first had the image of her brother, naked, pop into her head. This image was followed by the thought: "Why did I just imagine that?" and another thought: "Am I secretly turned on by my brother?" and another thought: "Am I some sort of sick pedophile or incestuous pervert?" The only conclusion she could arrive at for all of these questions was "yes." In the weeks that followed, she did all she could to avoid having the thoughts, or at least prove them wrong. She mentally scanned her groin area for any sign of physical attraction whenever she was near her brother, and always seemed to notice a sensation there that she assumed was evidence of sexual arousal. She avoided all physical contact with her brother. She actually became quite cold towards him, trying not to smile when looking at him, which she thought might be an indication that she was trying to seduce him. She also started to avoid looking at little children in general, to prevent what she was certain was her secret sexual attraction to children. Jaya continued on as best she could, living with the secret knowledge that she was a monster.

But her negative thoughts about herself didn't stop with just these intrusive sexual fears. She felt as if she couldn't really do anything right. When she first got a boyfriend in 8th grade, she was riddled with thoughts that she didn't really love him and was, in fact, an awful girlfriend. When she borrowed her friend's notes for a class, she was convinced she was a cheater without any ethics. Whenever she became annoyed at her parents, she worried about what an ungrateful daughter she was. It often seemed to her there was no limit to her awfulness.

When Jaya finally had enough of it all, she decided to google some of the thoughts in her head. She was surprised to see websites about OCD pop up in her search results. An intake appointment with an OCD specialist further confirmed that this was exactly what she had been struggling with. She started to work with this therapist and learned that all of the negative thoughts she had been experiencing were intrusive thoughts and not "Jaya" thoughts. She came to view them as negative judgments resulting from OCD that she never did anything to deserve, and this helped her to minimize the importance of the thoughts. For the first time in her life, Jaya learned to identify her own thoughts and beliefs she had about herself and began to find her confidence.

Edward and "The Stealthy Alarmist"

Edward doesn't remember exactly when it started but, sometime in early childhood, he began to worry about dying. At first it was just at nighttime. Once the lights went out, he would lie in bed imagining that his heart might stop beating or his lungs would stop working. He would ask his parents to sit with him at night and reassure him everything was going to be okay. For a while, he tried to make his mom sleep in his room, which she did for months until Edward's father put a stop to it. Edward had to resort to having his Mom say a specific prayer with him every night before leaving his bedside. If they could say it "just right," Edward felt like it would make sure God would protect him through the night. When he first started school, he worried that his parents would forget to pick him up from school. So much so, that he experienced a panic attack before leaving home on his first day, prompting his mom to take him to the hospital for what she thought might be a heart condition. The doctors found nothing wrong, but the experience changed Edward. He spent his waking hours trying to stay as calm as possible and avoid having his heart rate accelerate. He avoided sports and physical activity. He would put up a fuss whenever he was asked to lift something, or go for walks, or do his chores. Edward's parents, frustrated by Edward's difficulty, often turned to calling him a baby and a wimp whenever he would refuse to do things. They would often force him into doing these things, which never went well, and usually resulted in meltdowns and shouting matches. Over the years, everyone adapted. Edward's parents gave in and let him avoid most things. And Edward internalized many negative things about himself, that he was just a baby and a wimp, that he was lazy and lacked motivation. He struggled periodically with different fears. He didn't like germs all that much and tended to wash his hands more than most. And he regularly worried about what others were thinking about him, to the point that he tended to avoid social gatherings. Edward eventually discovered that he enjoyed math, and this gave him some direction in life. He was good at school and ended up attaining a PhD. He married a wonderful woman he met in grad school. And yet, he struggled with a lot of issues early in adulthood. He thought of himself as a loser who wasn't good at anything other than math. He felt strong anger towards his parents, but he didn't know why. His wife observed him doing a lot of repetitive behaviors like turning light switches on and off and repeatedly washing his hands in a very specific manner. When she approached him about it, he reported barely noticing he was doing it. The couple also ran into trouble because Edward expressed reservations and fears about having kids, while his wife badly wanted children. They finally sought out a couples' therapist about the issue.

Luckily the therapist they found had long ago completed an internship at an OCD treatment program. She knew the right questions to ask and identified that Edward had been experiencing intrusive thoughts about harm coming to himself and others for most of his life. She also identified that Edward had been engaged in ritualized prayer, as well as rituals around "redoing" his schoolwork whenever he experienced his unwanted thoughts. It was identified that Edward had been struggling with OCD his entire life. As Edward engaged in proper treatment, he realized that there were lots of things he had always wanted to do, but that his OCD had stopped him from doing. Edward, the real Edward, had never been lazy or unmotivated or wimpy. He actually yearned for physical activity. There had been a stealthy companion on this ride he'd been taking through life. He knew there was a lot he now had to face. He didn't think his parents, who were pretty old school in their thinking, were going to be very receptive to this new story about OCD, but he was going to try to share it with them. And he had a huge number of lifelong OCD rituals he was going to have to challenge. Still, he felt excited. Hopeful. Maybe for the very first time, Edward was ready to take charge of his life.

How Can They All Be Living with the Same Disorder? What are the Common Threads of a Life with OCD?

No matter what unique story has unfolded from your experience with OCD, there are also some pretty universal qualities that come with OCD.

7

These are general traits that link the OCD experience for all of those that have it, and they transcend the "content" of your latest OCD concerns.

- You are preoccupied by one or more specific fears. These fears revolve around *possible* scenarios that disturb you in some way.

- You have tried unsuccessfully to disprove the existence of these possibilities. The fact that your feared scenarios are possible, and can't be completely ruled out, make them hard for you to ignore.

- You are prone to getting pulled into your imagination and having experiences that make it seem like your fears are coming true. These mental experiences include emotions like anxiety, guilt, disgust, and anger that make them highly uncomfortable.

- You spend a great deal of time trying to figure out the best way to respond to your fears and prevent the emotional discomfort.

- You have developed repetitive compulsive behaviors that help you to alleviate discomfort but cause problems in your life. These behaviors can be both physical (washing your hands, excessively rewriting things, redoing your steps, etc) and mental (problem solving, pushing away or suppressing thoughts, trying to keep your mind distracted, etc.).

- You avoid things in life to prevent your fears from being triggered.

- You tend to experience doubts about yourself, and your safety, and you give these doubts a great deal of importance.

- You feel the need to stay alert to danger, and don't like the idea of assuming you are safe and just relaxing.

- You find it difficult to accept uncertainty in the areas of your fears.

- You are hoping to remove any and all risk of your fears coming true.

That's a long list and if you relate to a lot of those bullet points, hopefully it feels good to know that you are not alone in your experience. But you might also be thinking to yourself "Wow. I'm doing so much wrong" or even worse "There is so much wrong with me." But that couldn't be further from the truth. As someone struggling with OCD, you possess a great many unique qualities that, when channeled for good, can bring you much success in life. The problems arise when you don't know how to manage these tendencies, which of course is the case because no one in life gives you this information. As someone with OCD, chances are you've spent a lot of time NOT sharing your symptoms with others, for fear of what they might think. And when you have shared, you've probably received some pretty unhelpful advice over the years. But fret not! Every day is a new opportunity to do things a little bit differently. And let's face it, you're reading this book right now, which is a first step! To further aid you in changing course, there is actually one more list of qualities that come with OCD just as important as the first. Below check out a list of some of the strengths that I have encountered in the people I've met with OCD:

- Highly imaginative
- Detail oriented
- Attentive
- Creative
- Cautious
- Responsible
- Conscientious
- Empathic
- Having a strong desire to be one's best self
- Having a strong desire to do good in the world

These qualities may not even be immediately apparent to you, particularly if they are all being channeled towards OCD rituals and avoidance at the moment. But trust me, that they are there. Just keep in mind that OCD is not a bad thing, and there's nothing wrong with you just because you have OCD. OCD is going to make your life more difficult at times, and it's definitely going to make your life more interesting. But it's also going to enrich your life, that is once you make peace with it, and learn to find your way in life as someone with OCD.

Chapter 1

Preparing for Your Travels (Understanding the Symptoms of OCD)

There are two important concepts that, as someone living with OCD, you're going to want to become somewhat of an expert on. Obsessive-Compulsive Disorder (aka OCD) is a mental health disorder that, true to its name, has two main components: 1) Obsessions and 2) Compulsions. You might think of your obsessions as the fears that you have developed as a result of having OCD. Your compulsions, meanwhile, are the various repetitive behaviors you've come to rely on in order to try and prevent your feared scenario from coming true.

Obsessions (Your Fear Themes)

Obsessions are specific, pervasive fears that you develop as a result of having OCD. These fears, however, are not your typical, helpful sort of fears. When your fears are working the way nature intended, they get triggered when there is compelling evidence in the outside world, something you pick up with your senses, informing you that you are in danger. So, the fear of dying in a car accident gets triggered when you see someone driving dangerously in your vision. And you don't experience the full-on fear of having cancer unless your doctor expresses concern and orders tests during your check-up. In other words, you only think about bad, uncomfortable, and scary things in life when required. Your OCD obsessions, on the other hand, are specific fears that take on a predominant role in your life, not because you are experiencing repeated, compelling evidence in the real world that you are in danger, but because, as someone with OCD, you are having repeated, absorbing experiences in your imagination that convince you that this *possible* scary thing is happening. These believable, imaginative experiences bother you, and capture your attention. And they convince you to do everything you can to prevent your feared scenario from happening.

10

Unfortunately, OCD obsessions always exist in an area of uncertainty in life, and so you can never 100%, completely eliminate them from the realm of possibility. This inability to completely disprove your OCD fears keeps you locked in an endless OCD cycle that keeps you "spinning in circles."

And this is how your obsession is born. It starts as a possibility in your head that bothers you. You engage with that possibility, and the more you engage with that possibility, the more prominence that possibility takes in your life. Whether you are thinking through the specifics of your fear, or staying alert for any evidence that your feared scenario is happening, or trying not to think about your fear, or avoiding something in life so that your fear won't get triggered, you are still engaging with your fear. It is always driving your behavior in some way.

Over time, your obsession becomes something of a story in your life. *I'm a scary or dangerous person. I'm terrible at everything. I will eventually become depressed and kill myself. I am going to die of cancer. I am someone who can't be trusted.* This story evolves over time as you constantly think about your fear, and continue to look for evidence of your fear, both internally, and in your environment. The problem with looking for "evidence" is that you always encounter information that affirms your obsession as possibly happening. Don't forget that OCD obsessions are always in an area of uncertainty. There is always something occurring that suggests you are worse at things than other people, or might have a health concern, or might be an untrustworthy, impulsive, or dangerous person. The evidence that these possibilities might be true is always present for all people. And if you look for the "evidence," you will find it. OCD also has a way of convincing you that the act of having thoughts is evidence of something bad happening (If I just had a thought about suicide, that must mean I'm suicidal) or the presence of an emotion is evidence that your fears are true (Why would I be anxious if I wasn't in danger? Why would I be feeling guilty if I was a good person?).

Unlike the popular use of the term 'obsession' as something you really enjoy thinking about, your OCD obsessions are things you don't like to think about. Because these fears are always in the back of your mind, and because

11

it is such an uncomfortable experience when these fears are triggered, you do all that you can to try and NOT think about them. Your attempts to not think about them, however, actually cause you to become preoccupied with your obsessions. And they become major themes in your daily life.

It is also worth noting that some obsessions might not feel like "fears" per se. You may have obsessions that make you constantly angry or agitated, or physically uncomfortable, or just "not right" in some way. No matter the specific details of the experience, the main point remains: you experience intense displeasure whenever you are reminded of your obsessions, and so you try not to think about them.

As someone living with OCD, you will struggle with one or more specific obsessions at any given time, and these obsessions will likely change and evolve over time. Your obsessions are usually unique to you, and if you were to meet someone else with OCD, you would find that, sort of like snowflakes, no two obsessions are exactly the same.

Just to exemplify how wildly obsessions can vary, consider the following list of obsessions organized by general obsessional themes. Keep in mind the list of obsessions is infinite and that this is just a sampling of possibilities.

AN INCOMPLETE LIST OF OBSESSIONS

Contamination Obsessions

- Fear of contracting a dangerous illness through touching "contaminated" objects and/or people, or from breathing in proximity to others
- Fear of putting loved ones in danger by contaminating surfaces with your own "dangerous" germs
- Fear of having to feel uncomfortable due to coming into contact with sticky or oily or "gross" substances
- Fear of becoming "dirty" or "grossed out" by touching something contaminated with germs or dirt, whether these things are visible or not
- Not feeling completely clean after using the bathroom and washing normally
- Fear of getting others pregnant by contaminating objects and surfaces with your semen
- Fear of becoming pregnant through accidental contact with semen
- Fear of "catching" something that is not contagious, such as autism, from breathing near an autistic person
- Fear of changing into someone or developing their personality traits through their germs
- Fear of getting high by accidentally touching someone who uses drugs
- Fear that your house is contaminated with lead paint
- Fear of moral contamination through contacting others with different attitudes/lifestyles

Perfectionism Obsessions

- A need to meet unattainable OCD standards in a variety of areas of life such as school, work, and extracurricular activities such as music lessons or sports
- Fear of performing poorly on a test
- A need to "master" things
- Fear of not performing as well as those around you
- Fear of not performing perfectly in social situations
- Fear of not getting things "perfect," whatever that might mean to your OCD
- Constant feeling that you are not devoting enough attention to certain areas of your life. This is constant because whenever you devote time to one area, you are automatically devoting less time to another
- A need for particularity in planning/organizing so the "right" amount of time is devoted to certain areas of concern

13

Just Right Obsessions

- Fear of not having things exactly the way you want them to be
- Urges to achieve a symmetrical feel in your body by always doing things equally with both sides of your body (for example, touching a person with your left hand after your right hand accidentally grazes them)
- Fear of physical discomfort from clothes not fitting "just right"
- "Just right" food urges such as needing your food arranged on your plate a certain way, needing different types of food to be separated, and needing certain foods, like berries, to appear uniform, and/or taste exactly the same
- Needing things to look "right." This does not necessarily mean clean or organized as you might never vacuum a room if your OCD says that vacuum lines don't look "right"

Scrupulosity/ Religious Obsessions

- Fear of upsetting or disappointing God and/or going to Hell
- Fear of accidentally selling one's soul to the devil through having the thought of doing so
- A need to confess (all small transgressions in behavior)
- A need to apologize (excessively)
- A need to have a well-defined morality that is beyond reproach
- A need to have completely genuine and absolute religious faith and devotion

Social-Related Obsessions

- Fear of being rejected/judged by others
- Needs to control the behavior of others
- Fear of the social consequences of having a panic attack or throwing up in public

Sensorimotor Obsessions

- Hyperawareness (excessive "noticing") of a biological function (one's breathing, heartbeat, swallowing, blinking, etc.) and a fear that you will be unable to stop noticing these things

Relationship Obsessions

- Fear that you don't truly love your spouse
- Fear that your spouse doesn't love you
- Fear that you will cheat on your partner
- Fear that your partner will cheat on you
- Fear that you're not being moral/ethical in your relationships

Harm Obsessions

- Fear that you are secretly a violent or homicidal person
- Fear that you may follow through with a violent impulse or urge
- Fear that you will engage in a violent act and end up in prison
- Fear that you will follow an urge to drown, suffocate, or harm your baby
- Fear that you are potentially a serial killer
- Fear that you will follow an urge/impulse to commit suicide
- Fear that you will become depressed and kill yourself

Fear of Being a Bad Person

- Fear that you will follow an urge to steal something from a store
- Fear that you are a racist person
- Fear that you will blurt out rude or offensive statements
- Fear of having bad thoughts about others
- Fear that you want to join a terrorist organization
- Fear that other people think that you are bad in some way

Panic-Related Obsessions

- Fear of having a panic attack that results in you being triggered by any slight symptom of nausea, dizziness, anxiety, increase in heart rate, and change in breathing
- Fear of losing touch with reality / detaching from oneself
- Fear of "going crazy"
- Fear that your throat will close up, or that your heart will stop, or that your lungs stop functioning

15

Health Obsessions

- Fear that you will develop cancer and not catch it as early as you could have
- Fear that a loved one, such as your child, might have cancer
- Fear of developing another dangerous or deadly condition
- Fear of becoming severely depressed and/or mentally ill at some point in the future
- Fear of experiencing cognitive decline
- Fear of losing your vision or hearing
- Fear of catching seasonal flu, developing allergies, and any number of other health concerns

Hit and Run Obsessions

- Fear of hitting someone with your car and leaving the scene without noticing that it happened

Sexual Orientation Obsessions

- Fear that you are a different sexual orientation than you want to be
- Concern that if you fear being a different sexual orientation that this means you are prejudiced

Existential Obsessions

- Fear of not knowing yourself/your identity/who you are perfectly enough
- Fear that life is not actually real, like in the movies The Matrix or The Truman Show

Magical Obsessions

- Fear that you will travel back in time
- Fear that you will revert back to an earlier version of yourself
- Fear that you will suddenly switch genders
- Fear that you will turn into another person

Other Various Obsessions

- Need to tell others every detail of every thought you are having
- Need to correct (when others don't say things exactly how you want them to)
- Need to know (the details of other conversations, or information around topics mentioned that you don't have complete knowledge of)
- Fear that you will follow an unwanted urge to do something harmful or embarrassing
- Fear of not having complete certainty around your own intentions in life
- Fear that you can't trust yourself
- Fear that you will lose control of your own behavior in some way
- Fear of making the wrong decision
- Fear of forgetting something that could be extremely important and will put you in danger
- Fear of doing something unlucky
- Fear that your thoughts have power and can cause bad things to happen
- Urges to count things and fears that you will never be able to stop counting things
- Fear of living with regret or guilt for the rest of your life if you make a mistake or cause something bad to happen
- Fear that you don't really have OCD and actually are a violent person, suicidal person, sexual deviant, etc.

What's the Connection Between All of These Varied OCD Fears? In a Word, Uncertainty!

All of these obsessions listed have one major thing in common. They all exist in areas of life that are inherently uncertain. There is no blood test to prove if you are a "good" or "bad" person. You will never be able to completely trust the accuracy of your memory. And it's impossible to know what, if any, germs are on the doorknob of your office. These areas of life, then, are all potential breeding grounds for "what if" thoughts (intrusive possibilities or doubts) that can't ever be completely disproven or "ruled out." And once you devote yourself to trying to fix, eliminate, or disprove a possibility or doubt in one of these areas, you learn that any success in this endeavor is only ever short-lived. All you can ever do is give yourself some temporary reassurance that the possibility isn't true. But the possibility will always return before long, reminding you that you haven't completely ruled it out. Even after all of your efforts, it's still possible. This is the nature of an OCD obsession. By committing yourself to removing a doubt that can never be completely removed, that possibility becomes more and more a part of your everyday experience. It becomes something more than just a possibility. It becomes a story being told and retold in your head about what might be going on. After giving it enough attention, that possibility can seem likely, and even start to seem true.

What Caused My Specific Obsessions?

In almost all instances, your OCD obsessions did not evolve out of a real genuinely dangerous and traumatizing life event. Your contamination concerns most likely did not result from an experience of contracting tuberculosis. And your fear that you might be a dangerous person did not stem from that time you stabbed and killed someone. Your obsessions can also change over time, seemingly at random, with one obsession periodically falling off your list of concerns, only to be replaced by a new fear you'd never previously worried about.

You may even find yourself being surprised by the content of your OCD fears and feeling confused by why you're finding them so disturbing. Your feared scenario might be something truly frightening like your daughter dying of cancer because you were not vigilant enough to identify a tumor early enough. But it can also be something that seems weird and inconsequential, like a pervasive fear that a piece of paper or trash is stuck to your back. Your fear might be of something fairly plausible like throwing up in public. Or it might be of something unlikely like traveling back in time. And yet the distress related to all of these obsessions can be equally intense.

For these reasons and more, it is usually unhelpful to go searching for a 'root cause' of your fears somewhere in your past experience. Many an OCD sufferer has wasted a lot of time and energy on this pursuit. Even in situations when a certain event triggered a new obsession, it's not possible to say that it *caused* your fear. Even if you started excessively washing your hands after your elementary school health class on germs, you can't say that the class caused the fear to develop. Otherwise, every student in the class would have also developed the same OCD fear. OCD is considered a biological brain disorder that you are born with. And while life may impact when and how your obsessions eventually surface, your OCD brain was likely with you all along, just waiting for the right opportunity to present itself.

All that being said, your OCD obsessions tend to be, at least loosely, connected to the things in life you hold most dear, whether that's your family, your morality, your health, the quality of your work, the opinion others have of you, or your overall comfort and safety. Your OCD tends to bother you about the things that are important to you.

Compulsions or Rituals (Your Attempts to Get OCD to Leave You Alone for a Little While)

As someone with OCD, you are living with seemingly random obsessions that are causing you to experience chronic doubts, anxiety, and discomfort. In search of relief from this seemingly intolerable situation, you end up developing compulsions or rituals (Note that these words are

19

interchangeable. Compulsions are the more technical term, but I'll be using the more informal word Rituals from here on out). Your rituals are the behaviors that you rely on to achieve some sense of relief and control. If your OCD bothers you about the possibility of coming into contact with dangerous or deadly germs, you might develop the ritual of washing your hands every 30 minutes using extremely hot water and following a very strict scrubbing regimen. This effort doesn't completely remove the uncertainty - there will always be some risk of contact with germs - but it provides you with at least some semblance of certainty. It also helps to feel like you are doing all that you can to remove the germs you may have touched, and as a result the behavior provides you with some emotional relief. That is, until the next time your fear of germs is triggered, and the cycle starts all over again.

As another example, if you are struggling with an obsessional fear of becoming "unlucky," you might develop rituals like trying not to think of the number 13 or never stepping on any of the cracks in the sidewalk, among other things. These actions do not in any way objectively guarantee you will have good luck. But the anxiety and uncertainty you've been living with are alleviated by these behaviors. They make you feel like a good, concerned, and diligent person. You feel like you're doing something about your predicament. Basically, your rituals work, to a degree. That's why you do them over and over again. And who in their right mind wouldn't do all they can to reduce the symptoms that are making them miserable?

There are, of course, some major problems that come with your rituals. They are repetitive and time consuming. They take over your life. They make it hard to do simple tasks. They may make you feel embarrassed and ashamed. They may even annoy the other people in your life. Most importantly, though, they give fuel to your obsession, and make you even more preoccupied by the random possible scenario that is currently monopolizing your attention. But we'll be talking plenty about all of the problems with rituals. For now, just keep in mind that there are very logical reasons why you do them.

It's important to recognize that pretty much any behavior can become a ritual. If a behavior becomes a repetitive habit that you "need" to do every time your fear is triggered, it's a ritual. OCD rituals include things like:

AN INCOMPLETE LIST OF COMPULSIONS

- Washing your hands excessively
- Washing your hands in a highly ritualized manner
- Excessively cleaning your belongings (laundry, wallet, phone, etc)
- Excessive and/or ritualized grooming (having to shower in a very specific way)
- Analyzing others for signs that they might be sick
- Avoiding others whom you think might be sick
- Avoiding foods you fear could cause you to become nauseous
- Avoiding certain clothing you have attached to something bad occurring
- Going back and repeating your drive to make sure you did not hit any pedestrians without realizing it
- Avoiding chemicals
- Doing things in a highly organized or scheduled manner (cycling through your clothes in a particular order, exercising a certain way and for a certain amount of time each day)
- Mentally arguing with and trying to disprove your OCD worries over and over again
- Mentally reassuring yourself every time your fears are triggered
- Arguing with or trying to disprove your OCD thoughts
- Seeking reassurance from others about the same worry over and over again
- Avoiding people, places, things, or activities that trigger your OCD fears and worries
- Trying to mentally block out or repress certain thoughts
- Saving an excessive amount of things "just in case" they might be useful in the future
- Repeatedly "checking" things like door locks, the stove, and other items to make sure they are secure and/or turned off
- Repeatedly "checking" your belongings like car keys and your phone to make sure they are still in your possession

- Walking quickly past triggering areas in your environment
- Avoiding all contact with triggering areas or objects
- Video recording yourself doing things so you can be sure you didn't do anything dangerous
- Praying excessively and/or in a highly repetitive or ritualized manner
- Waiting for a specific mental state (to feel a specific emotion or think a certain thought) before starting or ending a task
- Not physically exerting oneself in an attempt to prevent panic and/or feared physical symptoms such as rapid breathing, an increased heart rate, dizziness, or nausea
- Habitually scanning one's body for panic symptoms or other perceived signs of danger such as nausea, dizziness, or tightness in the throat
- Completing rituals based on lucky and/or unlucky numbers, colors, or words
- Whenever you have a "bad" thought, trying to fix it with a "good" thought afterwards
- Thinking through your decisions over and over again without making a final decision
- Doing things extremely slowly to avoid making any mistakes
- Repetitively checking your appearance in the mirror
- Excessive morning preparation (doing your hair over and over again, dressing and redressing)
- Requiring others to speak or act in a specific way
- Making sure that someone watches you while you are on your computer to make sure you don't do anything harmful or dangerous online
- Repeating certain tasks until they are perfect or "just right"
- Counting in your head
- Rewriting until "perfect"
- Rereading text until a "perfect" understanding is achieved
- Speaking a certain way
- Completing extra and/or excessive work to prove you are a good/competent person

- Completing certain repetitive tic-like bodily motions
- Staying in constant contact with loved ones, or tracking them via apps, to make sure that they are safe
- Making excessive doctor's appointments or repetitively seeking out medical advice from others to make sure you are not experiencing a serious health issue
- Researching online about pedophilia and comparing yourself to the descriptions you find
- Searching various health concerns online to try and reduce your fears that you have a serious health issue
- Avoiding knives, rope, pills, and other items associated with suicide
- Avoiding violent videos, images, and media
- Presenting as quiet, calm, and meek to prove to oneself and others that you are non-threatening
- Avoiding religious (crosses and mezuzahs for example) and/or sacrilegious (the number 6 for example) symbols to avoid having religious obsessions triggered
- Performing mundane tasks a certain way (twisting tops off of water bottles twice, plugging in your phone charger a certain way, petting your dog a certain way) to prevent bad things from happening
- Relying on "accommodations," a subtype of OCD rituals that involve convincing others to complete your rituals for you. This could include having others wash your belongings, having others answer your reassurance questions a specific way, having others be present while you are completing certain activities to monitor you and make sure you don't do anything "bad" or "wrong," etc.
- In general, depending on others...to prompt you to do things, to help you make decisions, to tell you that you are safe, and reassure you that you are a good person
- In general, engaging in repetitive behaviors to reduce your anxiety because you feel like you must always do something to get rid of your anxiety

23

Just as obsessions tend to change from person to person, your rituals are also unique to you. You've developed them based on what has been most effective for quieting the worries in your head. Your OCD, meanwhile, can be very hard to please (not to mention very good at coming up with new ways to make you worry), and so you've probably had to change your rituals over time. Whereas you initially just had to say your prayer before bed at night ("Dear God, I am deeply and thoroughly sorry for every bad thought I had about anyone today. Please forgive me."), you might now find yourself praying every time you have a bad thought, every time you hear an ambulance siren, and every time someone says the word 'death,' and now that prayer has to be repeated until you recite it with the most perfect and genuine feeling of penitence possible. Over time, you may find yourself adding sentences and even body movements to the ritual. And you may occasionally have to switch to completely new rituals when the ones you've been using have become too ineffective. All of this just to achieve the same effect and get OCD to leave you alone for a little while.

Complete Avoidance (When Rituals Aren't Enough)

Sometimes no amount of online research, asking others for reassurance, checking yourself in the mirror, praying, or washing your hands is enough for your OCD. In these cases, you may find yourself turning to another last-ditch effort to deal with your obsessions. Complete avoidance. This is when you entirely avoid any and all contact with your triggers, leading you to cut certain people, places, and things completely out of your life. One could argue that all rituals involve some aspect of avoidance (and that technically you could label your avoidance as a ritual), but complete avoidance does deserve its own mention. When you've decided to stop watching certain television programs or movies because of fears of seeing violent images, or turn down all invitations to events with children because of your OCD fears you might be a pedophile, you are now engaging in avoidance. At its worst, avoidance can lead you to cease contact with certain contaminated family members, drop out of college, quit work, and even stop leaving the house.

Mental Rituals (The Overlooked OCD Rituals)

When coming to understand your OCD symptoms, you will find it easy to identify the repetitive 'physical' rituals you perform to deal with your thoughts and feelings. Walking through a doorway repetitively or driving back home to make sure you didn't hit anyone are easily identified as excessive OCD compulsive behaviors. But you can actually perform repetitive behaviors with your mind. These are things that others can't see, and are just as much of a ritualized behavior under your control as are your physical compulsions. In order to identify the "thinking rituals" that you have control over, you must first know the difference between *thoughts* and *thinking*.

Thoughts or more specifically, **intrusive thoughts**, are the mental experiences that you can't control. As we will discuss further in the chapters ahead, your brain is a thought-generating machine. Just like your heart has its job of pumping blood, one of your brain's primary jobs is to come up with all sorts of creative thoughts. For now, the important thing to remember about these thoughts is that you don't have any control over them. They are triggered and then they happen. You don't get to control the random intrusive thoughts of your brain, any more than you get to control how your kidneys go about filtering your bodily fluids or how your small intestine digests your food.

Your **thinking**, on the other hand, is a behavior that you have some control over. After an initial intrusive thought pops into your head, you get to decide how much you analyze the thought, how much you problem solve, how much you review your situation, and how much you try to predict the future, among other things. You also, of course, get to decide how much you silently pray and repeat words and numbers in your head. These mental responses to your obsessions are all rituals as well. Consider all of the mental behaviors listed below. All can become repetitive and time-consuming behaviors that you feel the need to do every time your obsession is triggered. Here is a list of mental rituals to look out for, as you continue to gain an understanding of your OCD:

AN INCOMPLETE LIST OF MENTAL COMPULSIONS

- Suppressing your thoughts (trying not to think certain thoughts)
- Habitually reviewing the same thoughts or ideas over and over again. This is called "ruminating" or using one's problem-solving abilities on an issue that won't necessarily ever be "solved"
- Thinking through possible future scenarios in order to try and stay ready for and/or prevent a certain outcome (aka. worrying)
- Reviewing past events in an endless, unproductive manner
- Mentally reassuring yourself that your OCD fears are unfounded, whenever they get triggered
- Engaging in mental arguments with your OCD
- Evaluating your unwanted, intrusive thoughts each time they occur to try and decide if they are important and/or worth a response
- Constantly "checking" or analyzing your emotions to make sure that you are feeling the "right" way
- Monitoring your anxiety level as a basis for your decisions
- Staying alert, vigilant, and/or keeping your guard up
- Silently praying or reciting a mantra of some sort
- Silently counting
- Trying to organize your thoughts in a certain way in your mind
- Trying to think positive thoughts to neutralize negative thoughts
- Trying to "figure things out" in a repetitive manner
- Wishing things were different (this can actually become a repetitive thinking pattern that keeps you stuck and unable to move on)
- Intensely controlling your attention. This can either involve 1) focusing all of your attention on a particular concern that is bothering you, or 2) focusing all of your attention on other things out of a perceived need to distract yourself from your concern. Keep in mind that some attentional control can be helpful, and we will be discussing how to direct your attention towards productive pursuits rather than OCD concerns, but you also want to avoid keeping a tight grip on your attention and/or feeling like you "need" to control your attention.

Many of the above mental behaviors may sound like pretty "normal" behaviors. And the truth is, a lot of rituals would be "normal" behaviors, if you were to simply perform them here and there. But when you are struggling with OCD, you find it difficult, if not impossible, to perform the behavior once and move on. You find yourself relying on the behavior and utilizing it over and over again, every time you are triggered. As mentioned, OCD rituals are responses to your obsessions that you feel you HAVE to do. And even the idea of not doing these behaviors when triggered might leave you feeling exposed, helpless, guilty, disgusted, anxious, "not right," or just plain uncomfortable. As we will be discussing, however, a critical step in successfully managing your OCD will involve identifying all of your OCD rituals and gradually taking the steps to stop performing these responses to your obsessions. Right now, while they may be helping you to feel better in the moment, they are not getting rid of your problem. Your rituals are allowing your fears to grow, and keeping you stuck in a never-ending cycle of avoidance.

Accommodations (Rituals Involving Other People)

Many people with OCD end up involving those around them in their rituals. There are a number of reasons for this. For starters OCD can really make you doubt yourself. You feel like you can't trust your own memory, or that you are a danger to others in some way. OCD can also make you feel like you have to control your own environment to such a degree that others you live with could ruin the system if they don't learn the OCD rules. Whatever the reason, when you have OCD, it is extremely common to find yourself having a network of rituals, in which others must participate and assist, or at least go along with in some way. Here is a list of some of the typical accommodations that those around you can get pulled into doing.

AN INCOMPLETE LIST OF ACCOMMODATIONS

- Having others clean your belongings for you
- Having others make excessive purchases of cleaning products, bathing products, or fresh clothing to support your rituals around contamination
- Limiting the movement of others in your home, such as not allowing others in your room, or not allowing others to touch your bed
- Controlling the placement of items in the house to the point that others are not allowed to move things from their places
- Having others do things for you that would be too triggering to do yourself (for some OCD reason), such as plugging your phone into an outlet, or retrieving items from a particular room that OCD doesn't like
- Having others make phone calls for you or help you to avoid other triggering social interactions
- Having others purchase very specific foods for you (for example, limiting your diet to only fast food)
- Having others supply plastic utensils or paper plates for you
- Asking others to answer reassurance questions. These are questions that you have to ask repetitively in order to manage your unwanted thoughts and emotions. Examples include: "Do you think I hit anyone when I was driving today?" "Do you think this is cancer?" and "Am I going to be okay?"
- Asking others to watch you, or act as a witness, as you perform certain tasks to make sure you don't follow any unwanted urges. Examples include asking someone to watch you take your pills and make sure you don't follow an urge to take the whole bottle and overdose, or having someone watch you while you are surfing the internet
- Having someone say goodbye to you a certain way, or tell you they love you a certain amount of times
- Having someone complete a specific prayer or mantra with you before you go to bed
- Requring a parent to sleep in the same room as you
- Requiring someone to participate in your morning routine in order to help you get your clothing and grooming "just right"

How Do I Know If I Really Have OCD?

A lot of the OCD symptoms described so far may appear to fall under the category of general human experience. After all, it's pretty common to have worries. Who doesn't worry about what others are thinking, and take some precautions to avoid flu germs, and find uncertainty difficult to tolerate at times? There are a few things to consider when deciding if something falls under the umbrella of OCD.

OCD usually involves an irrational concern. When you have OCD, you become worried about something you don't want to be worried about and feel like you shouldn't be worried about. The concern is usually a low probability outcome (I am going to develop a deadly shellfish allergy even though I am not currently allergic), or even a bizarre outcome (something bad is going to happen if I don't put my clothes on in the right order every morning).

You have to complete repetitive rituals. Your coping strategy involves relying on certain behaviors that you believe you need to complete to deal with your OCD concern. These behaviors (aka rituals) must be repeated every time your worry gets triggered, and the rituals never seem to solve the problem once and for all. They always eventually need to be repeated.

The source of your discomfort is a small number of very specific concerns. Unlike general anxiety, you don't just worry about everything. You are typically focused on a specific one, two, or three concerns at a time and these concerns tend to follow you wherever you go and be the only things you worry about.

Logic tends to be unhelpful. When you have OCD, you don't find any sustained relief from noticing the irrational nature of your obsession. And someone else pointing this out doesn't help you either. At the most, this may give you some brief reprieve from your anxiety, but the worry inevitably returns.

The obsessions and/or compulsions cause significant distress and impairment. Lastly, for the issue to be considered a mental health issue, it must cause significant distress and/or impairment. This means that experiencing some brief periods of anxiety each day or feeling the need to wash your hands a couple times more per day than the average person would most likely not be considered a clinically significant case of OCD requiring diagnosis and treatment. However, if obsessions and compulsions are impairing your performance in school, or making it hard to focus when others are talking, or causing you to damage your body (red, raw hands from handwashing), or making life difficult in any other area, then you are experiencing impairment in life due to your struggle with OCD.

Further Treatment Options

When you are struggling with OCD, your treatment needs could range from simply needing a self-help book like this one to requiring extended residential treatment. Starting with this book alone is a great first step and could be all that you need to take your life back from OCD. If you find yourself struggling to implement the recommendations on the pages ahead, however, don't hesitate to seek out some additional support, and use the tools in this book in conjunction with formalized mental health treatment.

Therapy: When thinking about treatment for OCD, it is generally recommended that you begin by working with a licensed mental health professional, making sure that this is someone who specializes in the treatment of OCD (which is much different from the mental health treatment for other issues). An initial dose of treatment will typically involve weekly hour-long appointments. You'll want to make sure the person you see has the proper credentials (fancy letters like LPC, LMFT, LCSW, PsyD, PhD, DO or MD) and that they are trained to administer ERP (Exposure and Response Prevention) therapy. They also get some extra points if they can offer you ACT (Acceptance and Commitment Therapy) and/or Metacognitive Therapy in addition to ERP. Don't be afraid to ask the potential mental health practitioner how many cases of OCD they have treated (more than 50 would be a good number, but you may have to work with the level of expertise available in your area) and their success rate with their OCD clients (typically you will want to hear something above 75%).

Medication: Many people with OCD find that therapy alone is either too difficult or doesn't completely get them to the level of functioning they are seeking. In such cases, medication is usually recommended as a supplement to therapy. Medication can help to "take the edge off" the intense emotions you may be feeling, reduce the strength and frequency of your intrusive thoughts, and make the prospect of challenging your OCD fears feel more within your grasp. If you are struggling with the decision of whether or not to try medication, keep in mind that OCD is a real, biological issue. The brain scans of individuals struggling with OCD are distinct from those who are not. And for many, medication is an essential part of their treatment. If you feel like you fall into this category, don't hesitate to talk to your doctor (typically your primary care physician or a psychiatrist) about trying a medication, and follow their recommendations in this area.

More Intensive Treatment Options: One of the most difficult things about OCD treatment can be challenging your OCD fears all on your own between those weekly therapy sessions. In more severe cases, it may be too difficult, at first, to challenge your OCD fears when not in the presence of a supportive therapist. For this reason, there are programs out there that provide more intensive treatment than just 1 hour/week. Additional options include Intensive Outpatient Programs (9-15 hours treatment per week), Partial Hospitalization Programs (25 hours treatment per week), and Residential Treatment Programs (around the clock treatment). All of these options are time limited (usually 4-8 weeks) and provide a short, intensive intervention that helps you to turn the corner on your OCD.

So, as you embark on this journey, take things as they come. Your OCD, and your OCD treatment, have to take their course. The important thing is to keep learning, keep working, and keep growing, and to make sure you seek out the various levels of support you may need along the way.

Chapter 2
Going in Circles (The OCD Cycle of Avoidance)

Once you start focusing your attention on a possibility or concern that makes you uncomfortable (your obsession), and you start trying to do something to remove that discomfort (your compulsions), you are officially engaged in the OCD Cycle of Avoidance. At first, responding to the concern might seem completely reasonable:

"I'll just wash my hands and that will make the fear subside."

"I'll call my wife and see if she thinks I could have hit someone without realizing it."

"I'll review my feelings to prove I'm in love with my partner."

"I'll ask Mom what she thinks about the bump on my head. She'll know."

"Maybe praying to God will make me feel less guilty about that bad thought I just had about my friend."

But you soon discover just how hard OCD is to please. Your fears and uncomfortable feelings continue to get triggered on a regular basis, and each time OCD wants you to repeat that behavior that alleviated some of the discomfort last time. Soon, you're in a repetitive OCD cycle, going in circles.

The OCD Cycle of Avoidance is the same for all those living with OCD, no matter what your specific symptoms might be. It goes something like this. 1) You encounter a **Trigger**. This is a person, place, thing, or event. 2) This causes you to experience an **Intrusive Thought** related to your obsession. You evaluate this thought as important and relevant, which leads you to experience 3) **Unwanted Feelings** like anxiety, guilt, disgust, or a feeling that something isn't right. 4) You engage in a **Ritual or Avoidant Behavior**. The ritual is somewhat effective in removing some of your doubt, providing you with reassurance, and reducing some of your discomfort. At the very least, you feel like you are doing something about the "problem." And this cycle gets repeated over and over again. In visual form, it looks something like this:

THE OCD CYCLE OF AVOIDANCE

TEMPORARY RELIEF UNTIL TRIGGERED AGAIN

TRIGGER

Something Reminds you of your obsession

THOUGHT

A thought, image or urge related to your obsession enters your mind.

RITUAL/ AVOIDANCE

You perform a ritual or avoid something in order to feel more certain, safe, and comfortable.

FEELING

You feel at risk and uncertain. You experience emotions and sensations that cause you to believe your feared scenario is coming true.

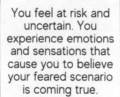

The 4 Parts of the OCD Cycle of Avoidance

Let's break down the four components of the cycle in a bit more detail. After this, you will be prompted to identify these four components as they relate to your specific OCD experience.

1. Triggers (The Everyday Events That Make You Worry Your Fears Are Coming True)

When you have OCD, there is nothing you want more than to not have to think about your fears and potentially get triggered into an OCD episode. And yet, everywhere you go, you seem to encounter reminders of your fears. That person you just heard coughing? They might have a full-blown case of bird flu or COVID-19. The way you just upset your son? That's just more evidence of what a selfish, awful mother you are. And that way you just randomly moved your hand in the direction of your sister's neck? Just more evidence that you are a psychopath who secretly wants to strangle her. The specific people, places, things, and events that remind you of the obsessions, which you are trying so hard not to think about, are called your triggers. Pretty much anything can become an OCD trigger. An item in your house. A certain place like school, church, or the office. A specific person. A random physical sensation. A word being spoken. OCD has a knack for twisting anything into evidence that confirms your fears. Here's a brief list of some of those OCD triggers. Maybe you'll relate to a few of these:

AN INCOMPLETE LIST OF TRIGGERS

- Touching a surface that you worry is not clean and/or sanitized
- Being faced with a choice or decision
- Seeing certain images or videos
- Making a mistake
- Behaving in a way that you worry might be bad or sinful
- Hearing certain triggering words
- Discussing certain triggering topics
- Seeing a part of your body or appearance you don't like
- Being faced with doubt or uncertainty
- Being faced with any small amount of risk
- Having to speak out loud
- Going to school or work
- Walking across a bridge
- Hearing your phone ring or give notification of a text
- Experiencing physical discomfort
- Taking a test and/or completing a difficult task
- Having a bad thought enter your mind
- Having a positive thought or experience (triggers OCD to tell you 'this won't last' or 'you don't deserve this')
- Someone being mad/yelling at you
- Encountering a certain triggering person
- Having a physical feeling that could be indicative of a medical concern
- Experiencing a sensation you fear could lead to a panic attack
- Having to touch something rusty
- Having to get a shot

35

- Feeling discomfort somewhere on your body that you fear you won't be able to tolerate if you don't immediately remove it
- Exerting yourself to the point of raising your heart rate and breathing rates
- Seeing an unlucky number
- Being around pills or other means for attempting suicide
- Becoming angry with someone (which OCD tells you will make it more likely that you will follow an urge to hurt them)
- Feeling something like low motivation or exhaustion that could be a sign you are becoming depressed
- Having a thought of suicide enter your mind
- Being around little children (when OCD is making you fear you might be a pedophile)
- Having to hold a sharp object (when OCD is making you fear you are a danger to yourself and others)
- Having a thought about doing something bad like stealing something from a store or pushing someone into traffic
- Having a 'not just right,' 'asymmetrical,' or 'incomplete' feeling that OCD tells you feel needs to be corrected or fixed
- Feeling a bump while driving that you fear could have been from running over a person
- Being near a person of the same sex (when OCD is making you obsessively doubt your sexuality)
- Having a loved one take a drive somewhere or do something else which could lead to an accident
- Having your partner get annoyed/angry with you (when you have fears of your relationship ending)
- Having to eat food that doesn't look or taste exactly "right"
- Feeling anxious

If you look closely at the list above, you'll notice that pretty much everything on that list is an everyday occurrence. But that's how OCD works, it uses everyday events to make you afraid. And this is why you end up getting your obsessions "triggered" so often. OCD can twist any object, event, or action into a reason that you should be afraid.

2. Intrusive Thoughts (OCD's Attempts to Warn You of Danger)

Intrusive thoughts play a critical role in the OCD Cycle of Avoidance experience. Your intrusive thoughts are your brain's attempts to alert you to the potential risk and danger that surround you. They are automatic, often unpredictable, and outside of your control. Experiencing unwanted, intrusive thoughts is actually a completely normal human experience, and people with and without OCD regularly experience thoughts they don't like, agree with, nor value. You get stuck in the OCD Cycle of Avoidance, however, when you decide to try and prevent and/or eliminate certain intrusive thoughts in the area of your obsession. This attempt to control your brain's thoughts is one of the main defining features of having OCD. One might even say that OCD amounts to a fear of thoughts more than a fear of actual, real life events. Think about it. How often does your feared scenario actually occur? Whether your obsession is around encountering deadly germs, or hurting another person, or forgetting to turn off the stove, how many times in the last year have you actually contracted a deadly disease, physically assaulted someone to the point of hospitalizing them, or burned your house down? The answer is probably 0. What you have had to endure, however, are non-stop, disturbing, or uncomfortable thoughts about these feared scenarios. The word "thoughts," keep in mind, is an umbrella term capturing a range of different mental experiences. The brain, being the wonderfully effective organ that it is, can present you with information in many different forms, all of which can be described as thoughts. Let's look at some of the different "types' of thoughts that you can experience.

SOME COMMON FORMS OF INTRUSIVE THOUGHTS

"What If" Thoughts

"Should" Thoughts

Labels

Memories

Doubts

Rules

Comparisons

Some of the Main Types of Intrusive Thoughts

The word "thoughts" is a big umbrella term that covers a wide variety of mental experiences, with regards to content and purpose. Many things fall under the category of Intrusive Thoughts. Here are some of the categories of thoughts that can become a part of the OCD Cycle of Avoidance.

- **"What if" Thoughts (aka: Predictions, Disturbing Possibilities):** Our brains, for very good reason, are adept at presenting us with things that "might" be happening. Think about how helpful it is to predict where the fish "might" be, the places where the lions are "possibly" hanging out, and where the fruit and vegetables "might" be growing. But when it comes to OCD, your brain likes to present you with disturbing "what if" scenarios specifically related to your fears. "What if there is listeria in my food?" "What if there is lead paint in my house?" "What if I'm starting to lose my mental functioning?" "What if I lose control one day and just attack a coworker on an impulse?"

- **"Should" Thoughts:** These are thoughts that constantly invite you to reject the reality in front of you and, instead, focus on an alternate, imagined reality that "should" have happened. These thoughts can get you stuck in mental rituals, reviewing what caused the outcome that "should not" have happened, and what you could have done differently to ensure the outcome that "should" have happened. At best, "should" thoughts are an unhelpful distraction from the real world. At worst, they consume your time and attention, and get you stuck in feelings of anger, anxiety, guilt, and dissatisfaction.

- **Comparisons:** A comparison thought is simply the result of you noticing how 2 things differ. Poached eggs taste better than sunny side up. Michael Jordan in his prime would mop the floor with Lebron James one-on-one. This route to work is 5 minutes faster than that route. Many of the comparison thoughts you experience are the result of your honest assessment of things. But comparison thoughts can get into your head for all sorts of reasons. You may have heard them from another person, from the media, from a bully, from a teacher. Your

39

brain also likes to toy with random comparisons as part of its creative process. Consequently, you may experience intrusive comparison thoughts you didn't choose to have, don't like having, and don't agree with. You can even get stuck with a comparison obsession, where your brain is constantly comparing your performance to other people. This leads to intrusive thoughts like: "Everyone on the team is better at soccer than me." "Everyone likes my brother more than me." "I'm the slowest person at my job." In cases like these, your comparison thoughts can go into overdrive, leaving you with a constant feeling of not being good enough.

- **Labels:** Labeling (along with other similar processes like categorizing, describing, etc.) are integral to the experience of thought. In fact, all language is more or less a labeling system, with everything in life getting assigned its own word (in both sound and written form). Our brains are constantly categorizing and labeling in order to make our lives easier, and safer. These thoughts give us mental shortcuts. Often, these labels end up ascribing a value judgment to the things being labeled. Oreos are yummy. Hard work pays off. I am a good speller. But, just as with comparison thoughts, we can experience intrusive labeling thoughts that we don't like having and don't seem particularly helpful to us. In this case, labels can have serious consequences for our mental health. Consider all of the following labels: "I am a bad person," "I am fat," "I am stupid," "I'm a violent person," and "My school is contaminated."

- **Mental Images:** Your brain can also utilize your visual imagination to make you have intrusive images. Your memories, your fears, your predictions; they can all take visual form in your head, even though these events are not actually taking place in the world around you. Again, the magic of the human brain.

- **Beliefs:** Beliefs are not technically a form of intrusive thoughts, but I include them here due to their importance. Beliefs are the underlying assumptions you are using to make your way through the world. While a lot of your other intrusive thoughts are more like possibilities that pop into your head, your beliefs are deeply ingrained in your psyche. They feel true for you at all times whether you are triggered and worried or not, and they guide your behavior in various areas of life. Beliefs can result from a thorough critical thinking process, or they can just sort of develop on their own. Beliefs can also vary in their flexibility. Some feel strong and impenetrable like a brick wall. Others feel like they could easily change as your life experience changes. No matter how strong the belief, however, be aware that ALL beliefs can change if you open yourself up to new experiences and information. Unhelpful beliefs can play a big role in your OCD Cycle of Avoidance. For example, if you have the belief "I can't handle anxiety," this will fuel intrusive thoughts every time you're anxious. You'll get that uncomfortable feeling in your chest, and thoughts like "This is something I can't handle," or "I have to do something to get rid of this feeling," or "I have to stop whatever it is I'm doing" will pop into your head. Other unhelpful beliefs that can lead to intrusive thoughts include "I have to be perfect," "All thoughts have meaning," and "Absolute certainty is achievable."

- **Memories:** Memories are thoughts about past events, often including mental images, that exist in your mind and can be triggered by reminders in the present. We have an amazing ability to "relive" these past events. When we experience a memory, it can draw from all of our senses and we can imagine the smells, textures, tastes, sounds, and images of the past even as if we are back in that place. Intrusive memories can become part of your OCD pattern when you have memories that you are trying intensely not to think about. Our memories are also extremely unreliable, and our brains can forget, distort, and even completely invent things in our memory, which can lead to ritualizing in an attempt to create certainty around our recollection of things. This is discussed in more detail in Chapter 6.

- **Rules:** Rules are rigid thoughts you choose to follow as a means of governing your behavior. They tend to include absolute terms such as 'always' and 'never.' Essentially, they cut out the decision-making component of your behavior in areas where considering multiple alternatives is either dangerous or unnecessary. Most of the rules we

41

choose to follow are important for our safety and success. 'Always look both ways before crossing the street.' 'Never cheat on a test.' 'Never put a fork in an electrical outlet.' Following these rules has real purpose and impact. We can find ourselves in trouble, however, when we choose to arbitrarily create and follow rules simply for the sake of having rules. 'I have to do my daily routine in this order' 'I run 10 miles every day at 6:15pm,' and 'I always wear this shirt on Monday' can interfere with living not only because they do not serve any substantive purpose, but because, once we decide they are rules, we can't change them even when circumstances demand that we do.

- **Doubts:** OCD is often called the Doubting Disease for good reason. Intrusive doubts can be one of the primary types of thoughts that you experience in the Cycle of Avoidance. Doubts tend to be questions starting with "Are you sure..." that pop into your mind after completing a behavior. They bring you to question your competence, your memory, your knowledge, and even your own experience. Examples include "Are you sure you unplugged the hairdryer?" "Are you sure you don't smell a gas leak?" and "Are you sure you didn't miss any questions on the test?" Doubts can also occur in response to the behavior of others ("Are you sure the doctor properly examined the CT scan?" "Are you sure the lead paint technician checked all the walls in the house?") and objects ("Are you sure the spaghetti jar made the usual popping sound when you first opened it?" "Are you sure the car isn't making a strange noise?"). When you develop a pattern of identifying doubts as important, and investigating every doubt that pops into your head, we call this "obsessional doubt." Your automatic, repetitive response to your doubts become a pervasive pattern that reinforces a general distrust in yourself.

3. Unwanted Feelings (How OCD Tricks You into Thinking Your Obsessions Are Worth Your Attention)

Thoughts alone typically don't demand our attention. It's usually those thoughts that trigger feelings inside of us that we find hardest to ignore. If the thought "I'm going to be fired" enters your mind and you don't feel any emotion with it, you won't be spending much time thinking about that thought. But if you have the thought "I'm going to be fired" and immediately experience a rush of anxiety symptoms and a guilty emotion, you're going to appraise that thought as being really, really important. For this reason, anxiety, emotions, and physical sensations play a big role in having OCD. When you are struggling with an obsession, it's because OCD has randomly linked a specific uncomfortable physiological response to a certain life concern. OCD might link a feeling of anxiety to the thought that the utensils and dishware in your kitchen might be unsafe. Or it might link a feeling of shame to the thought that you could be a bad person. These emotions then get triggered every time you think about the silverware in your house, or the possibility that you might have done something "bad." And, before you know it, you are attending to these thoughts left and right, whenever you experience them, giving them your full attention, and you have a full-blown obsession on your hands, due largely to that emotion getting triggered.

It's important to recognize that, with OCD, these feelings are randomly linked to your obsessive theme. This separates OCD from other issues you might be struggling with in life. When you feel sadness and grief because a family member has died, there is a real-world explanation for the feelings. In OCD, there is an irrational or exaggerated element to the feelings you experience. This random nature, of course, doesn't make the experience feel any less real. The presence of feelings like anxiety, guilt, and disgust make your feared scenario feel like a real threat in your life.

Note too that I'm using the word "feelings" as an umbrella term to capture experiences that extend beyond just your emotions. Let's look at all of the different bodily experiences that can be triggered by your intrusive thoughts:

43

UNWANTED FEELINGS

**Uncomfortable
Emotions**

**Anxiety
and
Panic**

**Intrusive
Urges**

**Feelings
of
Uncertainty**

**Psychosomatic
Sensations**

**Not
Just
Right**

Some Common Unwanted Feelings

- **Anxiety:** Anxiety is your body's way of preparing you to, quickly and effectively, deal with threatening situations. Your body doesn't want you wasting precious time thinking and decision-making when you are in immediate danger, and so it uses the powerful and visceral rush of anxiety to compel you into action. Anxiety brings with it a wide range of physiological changes (see below) all intended to be adaptive in a dangerous situation. The challenge for us modern human beings, in our physically safe and sedentary lives, is that the abstract, unending stressors of modern life trigger the same anxiety symptoms as coming face to face with a bear in the woods. And so we inevitably have to learn to accept and manage anxiety, which often feels like an added difficulty in our lives rather than an adaptive process. When you have OCD, your obsessions can trigger an anxious response whenever the content of your obsession enters your mind. And this anxious response can further convince you that your feared scenario is, in fact, an urgent and real concern that you must address. Furthermore, you may develop an aversion to anxiety itself. In which case you may be trying to eliminate anxiety symptoms just as much as you are attempting to prevent the feared scenario of your obsession. Take a look at the (incomplete) list of anxiety symptoms below and notice which you tend to experience:

☐ Restlessness

☐ A sense of doom/danger

☐ Rapid heartrate

☐ Fatigue and weakness

☐ Difficulty concentrating on anything other than the present concern

☐ Rapid breathing

☐ Sweating

☐ Trembling

☐ Tightness in the throat

☐ Tightness in the chest

☐ Difficulty sleeping

☐ Stomach issues

☐ Dry mouth

☐ Nausea

☐ Muscle tension

☐ Dizziness

☐ Shortness of breath

- **Panic Symptoms:** A panic attack is a brief episode of intense anxiety that includes more intense physical symptoms than a typical bout of anxiety. These symptoms can be frightening to the point of causing you to fear you may be dying or going crazy. Experiencing an initial panic attack can result in the development of a fear of having additional panic attacks, and you may begin to regularly monitor your body for any signs that a panic attack could be starting (which ironically increases the possibility you will have another panic attack). Many OCD sufferers have experienced at least one panic attack. But, perhaps more importantly, many individuals with OCD regularly experience low-grade panic symptoms that can leave them feeling constantly on edge.

- **Uncomfortable Emotions:** Your intrusive thoughts can also cause you to experience uncomfortable emotions. Your specific obsession will often dictate the specific emotion that gets triggered. Disgust tends to come with contamination. Guilt is often triggered by concerns with morality and God. And embarrassment and shame are often triggered by social fears. But keep in mind that OCD loves to mix and match things. It's not uncommon to experience guilt with contamination fears or a disgusted feeling with scrupulosity concerns. Here is an inherently incomplete list of human emotions. Take a moment to identify which ones are the prominent emotion/s you experience during your OCD episodes:

☐ Sadness	☐ Depression / Anger directed at oneself
☐ Anger / Annoyance / Agitation	
	☐ Embarrassment
☐ Fear	☐ Guilt
☐ Disgust	☐ Loneliness
☐ Loss	☐ Boredom
☐ Jealousy	☐ Surprise
☐ Shame	☐ "Not right" / Incomplete

- **Feelings of Uncertainty:** The thing that links all OCD obsessions is that they all exist in areas of uncertainty in life. OCD makes you afraid of bad things that *might* happen, and troubling possibilities that *could* be true. And it's always in an area of life where you can't 100% prove OCD wrong. Things like 'what others are thinking about you,' 'whether or not you might have an unseen health problem,' 'what God thinks of you,' 'if there are dangerous germs on a doorknob,' 'what your "true" intentions and desires are,' and 'what is going to happen in the future.' But OCD isn't content to just make you aware of an area of uncertainty. Pretty much everyone is aware on some level that things in life are uncertain. This awareness doesn't automatically lead to obsessions. And even in yourself, as someone with OCD, you don't worry and ritualize about every uncertain thing you encounter in life. You might be terrified of going to Hell but have no problem taking the risk involved in getting into a car and driving along the interstate. The thing that happens in the area of your obsession is that OCD actually makes you *feel* uncertain, which is a very different thing than just being aware of uncertainty. This feeling of uncertainty is something that you, as someone with OCD, are acquainted with on a very deep level. You are regularly forced to face the possibility of your feared scenario occurring to a disturbing degree that's not easily accessible to most other people. When you become scared that you might have cancer, you can very literally feel what it would be like to have an actual diagnosis and see your death on the horizon. You feel genuinely uncertain, as in, you really don't know how much longer you're going to be alive. And the same goes for any other OCD obsession you might be struggling with. Someone without OCD, on the other hand, never has to face these frightening possibilities in the same way. Sure, you could probably get someone without OCD to admit that they don't really know if they have cancer in this moment, and that they can't be 100% certain they're not going to Hell, but this would just be an intellectual exercise. That person would have an extremely hard time reaching the level of uncertainty and fear that you feel when your OCD is triggered. They wouldn't feel genuinely scared unless faced with a real threat to their safety. Your OCD, meanwhile,

47

can give you the experience of being in imminent danger wherever you may be, whether that's a bustling city street, a quiet room, a serene park, or a classroom.

- **Not Just Right / Incomplete:** Just right OCD is a subtype of OCD that veers slightly from other OCD presentations. When you are struggling with just right OCD, you engage in time-consuming and repetitive rituals out of a desire to achieve a complete or "just right" feeling. Conversely, when you resist the urge to complete these rituals, you are left with a "not just right" or incomplete feeling. Someone with just right OCD might wash their hands, not a certain number of times, but as long as it takes to get rid of the "not right" feeling. Just right OCD typically involves a fear that the incomplete or not just right feeling, and accompanying anxiety, will never go away if one's rituals are not completed. There is not necessarily a fear that any other bad consequence will ensue.

- **Intrusive Urges:** Some of your feelings can present as physical "urges" that show up in your body. Your OCD might make you feel the need to move your body a certain way, wash your hands a certain way, or even talk or think a certain way. And you might become convinced that your uncomfortable emotions won't ever go away unless you follow through with the urge.

- **Physical Sensations:** Physical sensations can play a major role in the Cycle of Avoidance. First of all, they can be the triggers that start the Cycle. For example, a feeling in your stomach can trigger your fear of getting sick. And a sensation in your head could trigger your fear of a "brain bleed." But physical sensations can also be triggered during the cycle as well. You could, for example, become scared that you might be attracted to the small children at your nephew's birthday party. This might result in you mentally "checking" your body for any signs of "attraction." Your attention shifts to your groin, and you inevitably notice a physical sensation there. You appraise that physical sensation as a sign of "physical attraction." This causes anxiety, and the sensation in your groin only seems to increase. In this case, the focused attention on that part of the body can either amplify a minor sensation that is always there, or it can cause your nerves to produce a sensation in that area. What's more, anxiety comes with a variety of physical sensations. Dizziness, tightness in the throat, queasiness, muscle tension, and increased body heat are all examples of sensations that can result from anxiety, and these sensations can be processed in a variety of ways depending on what you fear. The important thing to remember about "sensations" is that they are benign experiences that are not evidence of anything all on their own. A stomach sensation is not evidence of cancer. And a sensation in your groin is not evidence of attraction..

To put this all into even greater perspective, here are some examples of how unwanted feelings create convincing and triggering experiences, thus perpetuating the Cycle of Avoidance:

Robert has developed an obsessive fear that he is a pedophile. His primary strategy to counter the fear has been to "figure out" if he is attracted to young children. He hopes that if he can identify what he truly feels inside, he will be able to remove the fear from his mind. Whenever he is around children, Robert will "check" his thoughts, feelings, and bodily sensations in an effort to answer the question of whether or not he is a pedophile. He regularly notices a physical sensation in his groin that he judges to be sexual attraction. He also notices himself identifying some of the children to be more attractive than others, which he believes is another sign of the inappropriate and immoral thoughts and urges inside of him. Robert's "checking" strategy only results in him becoming more convinced that he is a pedophile, because rather than finding foolproof evidence to eliminate his fears, he finds feelings and sensations that "could" mean he is a pedophile. More than anything else, it is the sensations he repeatedly notices in his groin that make him believe that his fears are real and urgent. He makes the error of trying to search his feelings for the truth, and then relying on physical sensations for the answer. In reality, all manner of physical sensations can be experienced in the groin once one devotes attention to this area. And so these sensations do not provide evidence for or against attraction.

49

Makayla has developed a sudden fear of throwing up. She fears that the germs of others will give her a stomach virus. She finds that she can't sit in desks that have gum under them and that she has to leave school when any of her classmates look pale and possibly "sick." One morning, she sees someone who looks pale, and gets an initial intrusive thought that the person might have a stomach virus. After trying unsuccessfully to disprove the thought, she becomes convinced that the person really does have a stomach virus. She begins to fixate on the fact that she walked by this classmate when she first entered the class (or at least she thinks she did). She begins to feel pressure at the base of her throat. This is followed by a queasy feeling in her stomach. She feels like she might throw up at any moment. She leaves school and the physical symptoms eventually subside.

Katya has developed an obsession that she might be depressed and might want to kill herself. She meets some friends at a coffee shop and afterwards, the group of friends decide to walk to another friend's house. The walk involves crossing a bridge high above a river. Walking across the bridge with her friends, Katya experiences the thought that she might want to jump off the bridge and end it. She tries to push past these thoughts and continue walking because she doesn't want to appear scared in front of her friends. She starts to scan her mind for any urges that she might want to kill herself. This triggers more intrusive thoughts that she wants to end her life and be done with it. She looks into the waters below and visualizes herself stepping off the bridge. A feeling of terror overtakes her as she realizes she needs only to take a few steps to make it happen. She becomes convinced she's seriously suicidal and she's really going to do it. Once halfway across the bridge, she runs for the remainder of the distance, narrowly avoiding a panic attack. Arriving at the other side, Katya feels like she just barely avoided an actual suicide attempt. The experience has further convinced her she is suicidal.

You end up believing your OCD fears over and over again because the feelings you experience when triggered are so convincing. Basically, your feelings play a major role in your OCD, and they are often the #1 reason why you turn to your rituals.

4. Rituals and Avoidance (The Only Part of This Whole Cycle That You Have Any Control Over)

Finally, we come to your rituals and avoidance. So far, we have discussed how 1) a trigger leads to 2) an unwanted thought, which leads to 3) uncomfortable feelings. The most important thing to recognize about the first three parts of this cycle is that they are, more or less, outside of your control. There is only so much you can do to avoid OCD triggers. And you can't decide what thoughts your brain is going to have. And there is no way to ensure you will never feel a certain feeling. And yet, your rituals and avoidant behaviors are your attempts to do just that. They are your exhaustive efforts to control your thoughts and feelings. And these attempts have not been entirely unsuccessful. Your rituals provide you with a "sense" of control over your situation. Unfortunately, since fully controlling your thoughts and feelings is an unachievable goal, you become stuck in a never-ending cycle. Any control you do manage to gain over your thoughts and feelings is only ever temporary at best. And the sheer effort needed to achieve this tiny amount of control over your brain is unsustainable.

Your rituals are also the one part of the Cycle of Avoidance that you *do* have control over. While you may not get to decide what triggers, thoughts, and feelings you encounter on any given day, you do get to decide how you respond to those experiences. You get to choose whether or not you ritualize and avoid. And this choice has major ramifications for whether your OCD symptoms improve or worsen over time. This probably doesn't require a spoiler warning at this point: *Your rituals and avoidant behaviors make your OCD symptoms worse over time.* They send a message to your brain that you believe the OCD thoughts are a genuine threat, which in turn triggers your brain to keep sending you warnings in this area. Do your rituals long enough, and you eventually become afraid to find out what would happen if you don't respond. You become and more more dependent on these ritualized and avoidant behaviors.

Expanding Your Understanding: What Else is Going On?

On the next page, you will find a supplementary version of the Cycle of Avoidance. Now that you have an initial understanding of the way triggers, thoughts, feelings, and rituals work together, this visual offers a more complete picture of the path from trigger to ritual. As you review this diagram, pay close attention to how 1) your attempts to try and disprove your "what if" thoughts and 2) your absorption into the imagination inevitably lead to your decision to ritualize.

You might think of this diagram as showing a parallel process (your absorption into your imagination) that takes place while you are engaged in the Cycle of Avoidance. Your attempts to remove the unwanted stuff: the doubts, the what if's, the uncomfortable feelings, the risk, the uncertainty, etc., lead you deeper into your brain, and into your imagination. In your imagination literally anything is possible, and this is where you become convinced that the things you fear are coming true.

A DEEPER LOOK
THE OCD CYCLE OF AVOIDANCE

TRIGGER

1 SOMETHING CAUSES AN UNWANTED POSSIBILITY OR DOUBT (A "WHAT IF" THOUGHT) TO ENTER YOUR MIND.

4 YOU ENGAGE IN A REPETITIVE MENTAL AND/OR PHYSICAL RESPONSE UNTIL YOU FIND SOME RELIEF. BUT, BY GIVING THE OCD STORY SO MUCH OF YOUR ATTENTION, YOU HAVE REINFORCED IT AS A TRUE ACCOUNT OF WHAT'S HAPPENING. YOU MAY EVEN BE MOTIVATED TO BELIEVE THE OCD STORY OUT OF A DESIRE TO BE READY FOR THE WORST, OR AS A WAY TO AVOID FUTURE ARGUMENTS WITH THE "WHAT IF" THOUGHTS.

2 YOU APPRAISE THAT POSSIBILITY OR DOUBT AS IMPORTANT AND WORTH YOUR ATTENTION (OFTEN SIMPLY BECAUSE IT'S SCARY AND POSSIBLY TRUE).

3 EMOTIONS AND PHYSICAL SYMPTOMS CONVINCE YOU TO INVESTIGATE THE "WHAT IF" THOUGHT. YOU FOLLOW THE THOUGHT INTO YOUR IMAGINATION AND ENCOUNTER AN OCD VERSION OF EVENTS THAT YOU CAN'T SEEM TO DISPROVE. YOU ASSUME THE OCD STORY MUST BE TRUE. AND SEARCH FOR A RESPONSE THAT WILL PROVIDE YOU WITH SOME REASSURANCE, AND ALLEVIATE YOUR EMOTIONAL AND PHYSICAL DISCOMFORT.

FEELING

Seeing the Big Picture: Exploring Your Cycle of Avoidance

Now that you have a full understanding of how the Cycle of Avoidance works, it's time to map out your own unique Cycle. On the pages ahead, you'll find some examples of the OCD Cycle of Avoidance completed by four other people with OCD. They exhibit obsessions around 1) a fear of bad luck, 2) a fear of serious health concerns, 3) perfectionism, and 4) scrupulosity/contamination. Following these examples, you'll be prompted to complete the same worksheet using your own OCD symptoms.

THE OCD CYCLE OF AVOIDANCE

MARIA
LUCK
OBSESSION

TRIGGER

I see the number 13 on someone's license plate.

THOUGHTS

I experience the thought "What if this is a bad omen?" I realize I was thinking about my boyfriend when I saw the number. I experience the thought "I might have just caused something bad to happen to him."

FEELINGS

I feel scared by the thought that I might have caused something bad to happen. I am uncertain what the bad thing might be, and when it might happen. I feel intense feelings of panic and dread.

RITUALS/ AVOIDANCE

I try unsuccessfully to mentally eliminate the possibility that I've placed my boyfriend in danger. This makes the scenario seem even more likely. I try to reverse what I've done. I stare at something with lucky number 7 on it for 7 seconds. I say my boyfriend's name 7 times. I look down when walking around so I don't accidentally see the number 13 again.

TEMPORARY RELIEF UNTIL TRIGGERED AGAIN

THE OCD CYCLE OF AVOIDANCE

BELLA
HEALTH
OBSESSION

TRIGGER

I notice a hard bump on my neck.

TEMPORARY RELIEF UNTIL TRIGGERED AGAIN

RITUALS/ AVOIDANCE

I try to come up with an argument to prove to myself that I don't have cancer, but only become more convinced that I do. I research tumors online for an hour. I call my doctor and have to leave a message. I call my mother, who calms my anxiety by saying I don't need to worry about it.

THOUGHTS

I have the thought "What if it's a tumor?" I think about how much my daughter needs me alive and healthy. An image of my funeral enters my mind.

FEELINGS

I feel scared and uncertain. My heart begins to pound. I feel dread and deep sadness in response to the possibility that I could die soon.

56

THE OCD CYCLE OF AVOIDANCE

ALEX
PERFECTIONISM
OBSESSION

TRIGGER

I am building an IKEA table and realize I've been putting it together all wrong.

THOUGHTS

This brings on the thought that "I am bad at everything." I then think "Everyone who has tried to tell me I'm good at things is wrong," I have the thoughts "I will always waste my time trying to accomplish things" and "Nothing will ever work out for me."

RITUALS/ AVOIDANCE

I follow the thoughts and feelings into my imagination, where I am further convinced of the OCD story. I stop building the table and avoid returning to the task later. I act exaggeratedly upset to "let off steam." Others tell me that I'm perfectly capable and I argue with them. I feel like I've warned people in case I am ever trusted with something and screw it up.

TEMPORARY RELIEF UNTIL TRIGGERED AGAIN

FEELINGS

I feel ashamed and guilty. I feel angry that I was born so much worse at things than others. I feel scared that others place their trust in me.

THE OCD CYCLE OF AVOIDANCE

CALEB
SCRUPULOSITY/
CONTAMINATION
OBSESSION

TRIGGER

I am putting on a jacket when I have the thought "God is dead."

TEMPORARY RELIEF UNTIL TRIGGERED AGAIN

RITUALS/ AVOIDANCE

I am convinced I am dirty and must respond. I put the jacket in storage and decide not to go near it. I wash my hands to cleanse myself. I say a prayer apologizing to God for the thought. I try to keep my mind occupied for the rest of the day so that the thought won't pop back into my head.

THOUGHTS

I have the thoughts "I've just jinxed myself" and "My jacket is now "jinxed." I also have the thought "I am an awful and 'dirty' person."

FEELINGS

I feel ashamed and guilty. I feel a disgusted feeling about myself as if I am "contaminated" or "dirty."

Exercise: My OCD Cycle of Avoidance

Let's identify how your own specific OCD symptoms work together to create the cycle you've found yourself in. Make some copies of the blank Cycle of Avoidance worksheet below and see if you can identify as many details about your own OCD as possible. Feel free to make multiple versions if you are struggling with multiple obsessions. If, for example, you are experiencing contamination fears and scrupulosity (religious) fears, you can complete a separate cycle for each.

As you map out the patterns of your OCD, be sure to ask yourself the following important questions:

- Are your thoughts occurring in an area of uncertainty where doubts can never be completely eliminated?

- Do your triggered feelings play a big role in convincing you to pay attention to your intrusive thoughts?

- Will your rituals ever eliminate your intrusive unwanted possibilities and doubts once and for all?

- How long have you been trying to use your rituals to solve this problem?

- Will you ever succeed in controlling your thoughts and feelings?

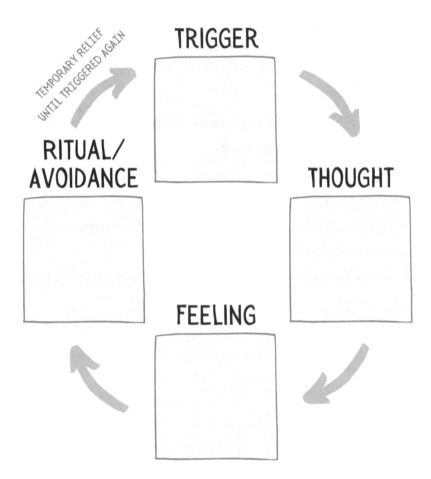

Understanding The Cycle (And Why You Find Yourself Stuck in It)

So, you're stuck in a cycle. That much is clear. You've been trying to achieve the impossible by:

- **Seeking Certainty** where it can never be completely achieved

- **Avoiding Risk** when there is no way to completely remove it

- **Removing Discomfort** even though life will never be free from discomfort

There are probably multiple reasons why you continue to engage in this cycle, and it's important to bring these reasons to the surface. As someone living with OCD, you are going to have some natural ambivalence when it comes to your relationship with this cycle. On the one hand, you obviously don't want to let your OCD control your life in this way, but on the other hand, there is a part of you that wants to keep trying to achieve those impossible goals listed above. The question you have to ask yourself before "*How* do I break free of this cycle?" is "Do I even *want* to break free from this cycle." Below I've listed some of the common reasons why people get caught up in the OCD Cycle of Avoidance. See if any of these describe your own motivations for continuing to attend to your OCD thoughts and feelings and engage in your rituals.

- You think that your OCD thoughts are important and deserve your attention simply because they are threatening, upsetting, or disturbing.

- You feel like you have to figure out if your OCD thoughts are true each time they are triggered.

- You habitually follow the thoughts into your imagination, where you are inevitably convinced your fears are coming true and/or you are in a high stakes situation.

- You are scared the thoughts and feelings will ruin your day or take away your happiness in some way if you don't eliminate them.

61

- You hope that if you keep thinking about things (aka mentally ritualizing), you will be able to find the one argument to finally prove your fears wrong and end your worries once and for all.

- You want to challenge OCD, but you also want to keep a few rituals in your back pocket for when your anxiety gets to a certain level.

- It feels unsafe to commit to an overall plan of resisting rituals, and you would rather decide on a case-by-case basis when to challenge your OCD.

- You're open to reducing rituals and avoidance but only if you can be certain you are not in danger before you do so.

- You want to keep your guard up and stay ready for danger.

- You have developed a habit of seeing possibilities and doubts as important events requiring your attention.

- You are unwilling to place your trust in your ability to instinctually respond to danger when it happens, and feel like you have to always be prepared for difficult events in advance.

- You want to continue to check in on your anxiety level to gauge how much to trust your OCD worries, and you feel like your anxiety is a good judge of danger.

- In the case of fears involving scrupulosity or morality, you believe that giving yourself permission to stop ritualizing would equate to being a bad person who no longer cares.

- In the case of perfectionism, you think that giving up on your rituals will make you a lazy person who has given up or quit.

If any of these reasons are the ones keeping you stuck in your Cycle of Avoidance, be sure to take note of them. As you consider changing your relationship with OCD, maintaining any of these "reasons" for ritualizing will be a barrier to success. But if you can truly commit yourself to this process of challenging OCD, and let go of all the reasons above that have been keeping you stuck, you are going to succeed in getting your life back.

Breaking The Cycle (Exposing Yourself to the Things You've Been Avoiding)

The difficult truth about having OCD is that, once you develop an obsession, you don't ever get to go back to that carefree time before you had that obsession. OCD has caused you to worry about something, and now it has become a theme in your thinking. You're going to have to figure out how to deal with that concern.

This leaves you at a crossroads, and there are two possible paths laid out before you.

Path A: You can try to ritualize, escape, and avoid to deal with the fears and doubts. You can try to achieve lasting 100% certainty about your obsession and try to control your intrusive thoughts and feelings. In other words, you can absolutely choose the OCD Cycle of Avoidance.

Or you can consider your other available option…

Path B: You can stop trying to achieve the impossible. You can give up trying to prove your fears and doubts wrong. You can choose to accept the thoughts, doubts, and disturbing possibilities your brain will sometimes conjure up, and the negative emotions that those thoughts might make you feel. You can choose to accept the existence of the inevitable sliver of uncertainty in the area of your obsession. And instead of turning to rituals to try and remove it, put your energy towards other things.

As difficult as this second path may sound right now, this is the alternative to the Cycle of Avoidance. There is, unfortunately, no *Path C,* where you get to overcome your obsessions and not have to experience any discomfort in the process. The path to feeling better will require you to go directly through the things in life that have been making you anxious and uncomfortable. You're going to have to do things that don't feel "right" or "safe." You may feel less in control at times. And you'll have to experience some emotional and physical discomfort.

What this basically means is that, in order to escape the Cycle of Avoidance, you will invariably have to **expose** yourself to the people, places, thoughts, feelings, and situations you have been unsuccessfully trying to completely eliminate from your life. This idea of **exposure** is one of the most important concepts in OCD treatment. From here on out, this book will take you through a process of gradually increasing the amount of time you spend exposed to your triggers while gradually reducing the number of rituals you do to try and eliminate the thoughts and feelings that get triggered. The key term here is 'gradual. You don't have to stop all of your OCD rituals tomorrow. And you don't have to face all of your fears by the end of the week. By engaging in this exposure process in a gradual manner, this journey will in actuality be much less scary than it might sound right now.

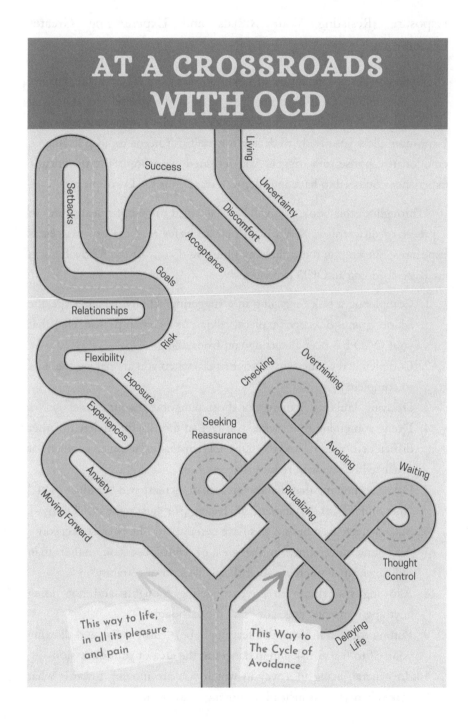

Exposure (Resisting Your Rituals and Experiencing Greater Discomfort)

Exposure is the foundation of treatment for anything involving anxiety or fear (including OCD). It involves "exposing" yourself to triggering situations while not doing anything to escape, avoid, or ritualize in response. Exposures allow your body to decide for itself if it needs to keep having an emotional response to a trigger. And repeated exposure is the therapeutic experience you need to have in order to reduce your OCD symptoms.

Throughout this book, you will be challenged to complete exposures in a variety of different ways. We won't always refer to these experiences as exposures, but keep in mind that any time you do any of the following, you are basically doing an OCD exposure:

1. Completing a task (engaging in a triggering activity, taking a specific action, going to a specific place, talking to a certain person, etc.) that your OCD has been deterring you from doing
2. Completely resisting one of your rituals when you are having the urge to complete it
3. Delaying, limiting, changing, or shortening one of your rituals
4. Doing something that makes you feel an increase in anxiety or other difficult emotion related to your OCD, instead of using an avoidant or ritualized behavior to reduce that emotion
5. Doing something that makes you feel an increase in a "not just right," "incomplete," or "asymmetrical" feeling (for "just right" OCD urges)
6. Making a decision before you have certainty it's the perfect decision
7. Accepting uncertainty in the area of your obsession, rather than utilizing a ritual to create an artificial "illusion of certainty"
8. Allowing your brain to have triggering thoughts and not doing anything to negate, erase, or "fix" those thoughts
9. Putting yourself in (what you fear might be) "harm's way" and allowing yourself to feel at risk and in danger in the area of your obsession
10. In general, living in a way in which you are moving towards what makes you anxious instead of moving away from it

Also be aware that exposures can happen in one of 2 ways: 1) **Natural Exposures** can occur when you encounter a triggering situation by simply living your life. Examples include, having to shake someone's hand at work (for contamination fears), having to write a paper for school (for perfectionism), witnessing a car crash (for harm obsessions), and driving past a church (for scrupulosity fears). When you are faced with these situations, you can either see them as just more opportunities to ritualize or avoid, or you can turn them into exposures by making the decision to follow through with the activity and resist your rituals. 2) **Planned Exposures** are another form of exposure. This is when you choose to purposefully create a triggering situation for yourself for the sake of treatment. It involves going slightly out of your way to seek out your triggers with the decision made beforehand to not ritualize or escape. Examples of planned exposures include purposefully choosing to take a driving route that involves crossing a bridge or passing through a tunnel (for driving anxiety), going to the grocery store with the intent of making small talk with the checkout clerk (for social fears), and walking around with a pocketknife in your pocket (for harm fears). Engaging in these experiments and repeating them allows your body to experience the triggering situation and see what happens. Overcoming OCD typically requires a plan of engaging in both natural and planned exposures.

What To Expect When You Resist Your Rituals and Reduce Your Avoidance

Exposing yourself to your triggers and resisting your rituals is the key to breaking free from the Cycle of Avoidance, but this is not an easy thing to do. In choosing to resist your rituals, you will be turning away that short-term "fix" to your unwanted thoughts and feelings. And you will be putting yourself in a place of greater uncertainty, risk, and discomfort. When you make the choice to resist your rituals and face your OCD fears, you are letting the thoughts happen, and seeing how things turn out. You are allowing the threat to exist. In essence, you are choosing to do something that will make you feel "worse," at least in the short term. Some of the things you may experience when you make the choice to not engage in a ritual:

- Increased feelings of uncertainty
- Increased unwanted, negative, or "bad" thoughts
- Increased uncomfortable feelings like guilt, anxiety, and disgust
- Increased negative thoughts about oneself
- Increased feelings of something being "not right"
- A strong sense that you are putting yourself and others at risk
- Feeling like you are doing something foolish, reckless, or wrong
- Increased physical discomfort
- Feeling vulnerable
- Feeling out of control
- A sense that a bad outcome will result if you don't ritualize

So why on earth would anyone purposefully cause themselves to feel this way? Well, here's the really cool thing. If you can start to expose yourself to your feared situations and not ritualize, you will be starting yourself down a path of major growth and change. You'll be letting all of those bad thoughts and feelings into your life, but you'll also be inviting in a bunch of good stuff as well. You're going to find your strength, and discover that you can handle uncertainty and risk, and that you can tolerate all of those OCD thoughts and feelings you've been trying to avoid. In short, when you decide to incorporate exposure and acceptance into your life, you start to get used to these things. They don't bother you as much. And you start to see that whatever life throws at you, you can manage it, and if something bad happens in the future, you'll be able to deal with it when it happens.

Habituation (What to Expect When You Engage in Exposures)

This idea, that things get easier with practice, is what we call habituation. And it's one of the long-term benefits you experience when you choose to eliminate your rituals and avoidance. When choosing to make this change in your life, you can expect to experience habituation in one of three ways.

Habituating in the Moment: This is when you expose yourself to a triggering situation and you experience a reduction in your intense emotional response, relatively quickly, during that exposure. Someone who is struggling with contamination fears and keeping their hands away from their face at all times, might complete an exposure by placing one of their hands on their cheek. Upon first starting this exposure, the person may experience a spike in anxiety and fear. They may suddenly experience intrusive images of germs, intrusive thoughts of contracting a virus, and even physical symptoms of nausea and dizziness. If they are able to stick with this exposure and keep their hand held on their cheek, these symptoms may gradually dissipate in the moment, to the point that every 10-15 minutes they notice the discomfort feeling a little less intense.

Habituating Over Time: For many with OCD, habituating in the moment doesn't always happen, or, if it does, they only experience a mild reduction in symptoms in the moment. This is where the importance of repeated exposure comes into play. If the person with contamination concerns above places their hand on their cheek and feels pretty anxious for a full 30 minutes, their arm may eventually tire, and they may have to end the exposure without having habituated during the exposure. And yet, habituation or not, exposures should be repeated to really overcome a fear. This person will have to set aside a time each day to do this exposure. In this situation, they can expect to experience long-term habituation, with the exposure gradually becoming easier week to week from repeated exposure.

Increasing Tolerance: A small group of people with OCD will report that, in the case of one of their obsessions, they have a particularly stubborn emotional response to a trigger. They don't habituate in the moment and also report not experiencing long-term habituation even after committing to exposures over an extended period of time. It bears mentioning that for many in this group, there may still be some avoidance and mental rituals being maintained and they aren't able to completely expose themselves to their thoughts and feelings. That being said, it's entirely possible that there is a very

69

small subset of severe obsessions that are much slower to respond to exposure therapy. In these cases, exposures are still recommended, but "habituation" is going to look slightly different. In response to exposures, you may have less of a decrease in discomfort and more of an increase in your tolerance for the discomfort. Your exposures may simply involve gradually increasing the amount of time that you can tolerate your trigger, even though the discomfort continues. Your gradually increasing inner strength and courage will be the thing that makes the exposures more tolerable over time. And, if the motivation exists, you will find this inner strength and courage. But again, for a vast majority of OCD sufferers, habituation is an expected reality of treatment when all rituals and avoidant behaviors are identified and removed, with the only real difference between individuals being how quickly habituation occurs.

Exercise: Mailing Out Some Postcards

On the next few pages, you will find some activities for starting to reverse the OCD Cycle of Avoidance. First, a postcard to share with your future self, identifying some of your current thoughts about OCD as you embark on this journey. Second, a postcard for writing out some of the initial steps you'd like to take to challenge your OCD. Lastly, you'll find a list of some important principles to remember as you work through this book. Consider making a copy of this page and placing it where you will be able to refer to it on a daily basis.

Write a postcard to your future self. How is your current Cycle of Avoidance impacting you? How do you feel as you embark on this journey of change? Hopeful? Scared? Unsure what to think? Any hopes and predictions for this journey?

_____
_____
_____
_____
_____
_____

To: future me

_____

From: me today
_____
_____
_____
_____
_____

your
ADVENTURE
awaits

Use this postcard to identify some initial steps you can take to challenge your current rituals and avoidance. Be sure to stick to some modest steps that you feel confident you can start to practice right now.

_____
_____
_____
_____
_____
_____
_____
_____
_____
_____
_____
_____

"DO ONE THING EVERY DAY THAT SCARES YOU."

-Eleanor Roosevelt

My Travel Plans

WORDS TO REMEMBER FOR THE VOYAGE AHEAD

THOUGHTS ONLY HAVE AS MUCH POWER AS I GIVE THEM

Responding to my thoughts. Trying to avoid having them. Doing rituals to eliminate them. Arguing with them; These actions all make my thoughts a bigger deal than they need to be.

THOUGHTS ARE JUST THOUGHTS

They can be scary. They can be convincing. They can be powerful. They can be offensive and at odds with my values. They can be critical and judgmental. They can even include imagery and physical sensations. No matter what, I must remember. Thoughts are just thoughts.

I CAN HANDLE ANXIETY AND OTHER UNCOMFORTABLE EMOTIONS

They pass with time all on their own and do not require a response on my part.

I DON'T HAVE TO AUTOMATICALLY BELIEVE MY FEELINGS

Just because I'm feeling a negative emotion like anxiety or guilt or disgust or anger does not mean there is a good reason for me to be feeling it. It does not mean that I am doing anything wrong or that there is something in my life that needs to be fixed.

I HAVE TO FEEL UNCOMFORTABLE EMOTIONS ON PURPOSE TO CHALLENGE MY OCD

Feeling this way means that I am doing a good job at challenging my OCD, and that I am bettering myself and improving my situation. I can feel good about the job that I am doing even when I'm feeling bad.

MY OCD WILL HAVE ITS UPS AND DOWNS

I will have good and bad days, weeks, and even months. This is part of Living With OCD. This is something I can handle by remembering that sometimes I just need to rest and take care of myself. With practice, I will make the good periods better and longer, and the bad periods less bad and shorter.

AVOIDANCE STRENGTHENS FEAR

Every time I engage in rituals and avoidant behavior in response to my OCD fears, I am communicating to my OCD that I believe I have something to fear.

EXPOSURE (WHILE RESISTING RITUALS) WEAKENS FEAR

Just as rituals and avoidant behavior strengthen your OCD fears, purposefully exposing yourself to your OCD triggers, thoughts, and feelings, while resisting your rituals, gradually reduces your fear.

HABITUATION OCCURS WITH TIME

Challenging OCD is difficult and scary at first. But through repeated exposure to my triggers, my body will habituate and the uncomfortable emotions will become less intense.

Available for download at *https://pittsburghocdtreatment.com/publications/the-ocd-travel-guide/*

Chapter 3

Map Out the Course of Your Adventure (How to Ignore the OCD Misdirection and Set Your Own Coordinates)

Managing your OCD will require the occasional course correction. There will be times when you look around at your life and realize you've been spending far too much time attending to intrusive thoughts and feelings, and not enough time living in the world outside of your head. And yet, despite your best intentions, it can be very confusing trying to figure out how to escape the OCD thinking loops and repetitive rituals that characterize your life once OCD has taken over.

This confusion actually makes perfect sense. When you fall into a pattern of habitually responding to intrusive "what if" thoughts and doubts (about your memory, about your morality, about your intentions, about your safety, etc.), it can lead you to become confused about a number of things::

- Who you are and what's important to you
- What is happening in reality vs. what is happening in your imagination
- The full scope of your rituals, mental and physical, that are keeping you stuck in the Cycle of Avoidance
- What options you have other than your rituals

But you are not fated to stay confused about these things forever. Once you start to reverse that habit of following the what if's and the doubts into your imagination, you're going to discover that your confidence, and trust in yourself, have been there all along, just waiting for you to notice. In this chapter, you'll be mapping out the current landscape of things. You're going to take note of the thoughts and feelings that tend to send you off course, and the choices you have throughout your day to either go down the path of

74

OCD avoidance and confusion, or move towards the world of your senses outside of your head. Basically, you're going to realize that you have choices, and develop a better sense of what those choices are.

On the next page, you will find the OCD Detours worksheet. This exercise uses Exit Signs to represent the intrusive thoughts and feelings that capture your attention. You might think of these exit signs as your brain's attempts to alert you to possibilities. The Exit Ramps, meanwhile, represent the turns you take whenever you decide to respond to those thoughts and feelings. Your behavioral responses literally take you down a divergent path from where you had previously been going.

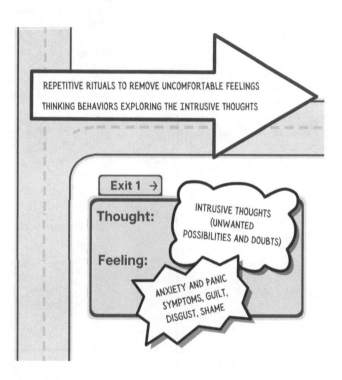

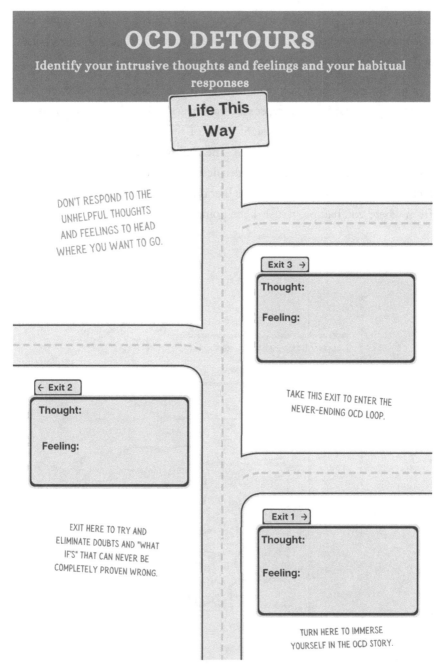

OCD DETOURS

Identify your intrusive thoughts and feelings and your habitual responses

Life This Way

DON'T RESPOND TO THE UNHELPFUL THOUGHTS AND FEELINGS TO HEAD WHERE YOU WANT TO GO.

Exit 3 →

Thought:

Feeling:

TAKE THIS EXIT TO ENTER THE NEVER-ENDING OCD LOOP.

← Exit 2

Thought:

Feeling:

EXIT HERE TO TRY AND ELIMINATE DOUBTS AND "WHAT IF'S" THAT CAN NEVER BE COMPLETELY PROVEN WRONG.

Exit 1 →

Thought:

Feeling:

TURN HERE TO IMMERSE YOURSELF IN THE OCD STORY.

Available for download at *https://pittsburghocdtreatment.com/publications/the-ocd-travel-guide/*

To complete the worksheet, you will have to 1) identify some of the thoughts and feelings that repeatedly lead you off track (the Exit Signs), and 2) the various habitual responses you have developed to the thoughts and feelings (the Exit Ramps).

Exit Signs and Bad Directions (Learning to Recognize the Thoughts and Feelings Associated with your OCD Patterns)

To start things off, let's look at Jeff, a 34-year-old man struggling with an OCD harm obsession (he fears he has secret impulses to harm other people). Jeff has completed the first exit sign by detailing some of the thoughts and accompanying feelings that repeatedly grabs his attention. Jeff identified that he experiences the intrusive "what if" thought that he might have secret violent urges, and that he could act on these urges with his loved ones. When he has these thoughts, he becomes uncertain, anxious, and fearful.

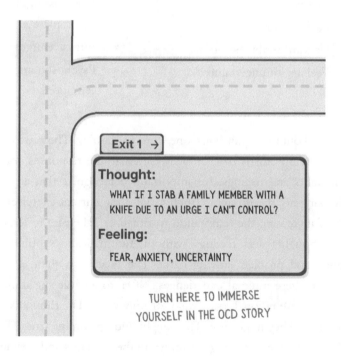

Exit 1 →

Thought:

WHAT IF I STAB A FAMILY MEMBER WITH A KNIFE DUE TO AN URGE I CAN'T CONTROL?

Feeling:

FEAR, ANXIETY, UNCERTAINTY

TURN HERE TO IMMERSE
YOURSELF IN THE OCD STORY

In order to map out your own patterns, you'll need to start by identifying some of the intrusive thoughts and feelings that repeatedly grab your attention and get you ritualizing. Find a sheet of paper or print out a copy of the OCD Detours worksheet, and you can begin recording thoughts and feelings for the exit signs. If you're having trouble with this first step, take a minute to review the types of thoughts and feelings discussed in Chapter 2.

Types of Thoughts

- "What if" thoughts
- "Should" thoughts
- Comparisons
- Labels
- Mental images

- Beliefs
- Memories
- Rules
- Doubts

Types of Feelings

- Anxiety
- Panic symptoms
- Uncomfortable emotions
- Feelings of uncertainty

- Not "just right" / Incomplete
- Intrusive urges
- Psychosomatic sensations

As you fill out those exit signs, one word of warning. The key to managing your OCD symptoms is to eventually eliminate the responses you have to these thoughts and feelings. It's important to recognize that any time you start "looking at" the thoughts (such as with the current exercise), you run the risk of increasing the temptation to ritualize. Take care to identify your intrusive thoughts and feelings without automatically slipping into the ruminating and problem-solving habit. The goal is to shine a temporary spotlight on these internal experiences, NOT to analyze the thoughts and decide if they are rational, true, valid, or important. The thoughts might be based on fact. They might not. They might end up coming true. They might not. The criteria you are using is simply: do the thoughts and feelings trigger

78

repetitive and time-consuming behaviors that don't accomplish anything in the real world? If so, add them to the list. No additional analysis needed.

If you continue to find yourself struggling to identify relevant thoughts and feelings, take a look at the list below which details some of the common intrusive thoughts that occur with various obsessive themes.

Contamination
- I'm dirty. That object is dirty. That place is dirty. That person is dirty.
- What if there are dangerous germs on my wallet?
- That food doesn't look right. Could it be contaminated with listeria?
- What if that the doorknob has the AIDS virus on it?
- What if I missed a spot washing my hands? I better rewash them.
- I have to avoid that spot on my bedroom floor because a shirt that touched that contaminated boy in school once fell on that spot.

Fear of Harming Oneself or Others
- Did I do something to harm myself and forget I did it? I feel like I taste aspirin in my mouth. Did I overdose on pills?
- Do I want to harm my family? Why did I point a knife in the direction of my Mom?
- Why am I mad at my husband? Is that my violent side coming out?
- Why am I feeling such low motivation? Am I getting depressed? Is this going to be the time for my depression to finally hit? Is it all going to lead to me eventually killing myself?
- Why did the image of myself hanging just enter my mind? Am I actually suicidal? Am I going to act on this thought?

Fear of Being a Bad Person
- Did I put something in my pocket when I was in that store?
- Why did that racial slur just pop into my mind? Am I a racist?
- Do I want to become a criminal?
- Why did I picture myself pushing that mother with a stroller into traffic?
- I only have positive thoughts because I'm "trying" to be a good person. My true thoughts are actually negative.
- Why do I always think about myself? I'm a selfish person.

79

- Good people don't have to "try" to be good like I do.
- I should never stop ritualizing and trying to remove the uncertainty. That would mean I'm a bad person who no longer cares.

Scrupulosity

- Why did I just think that blasphemous thought?
- What if I'm not devout enough? What if I'm not a true believer? I don't think my faith is strong enough.
- What if I secretly want to worship Satan? How would I know if I've sold my sold to Satan? Could it just happen if I think "Satan, I sell my soul to you?"

Hit and Run Obsessions

- Wow. I'm already at work. I must have totally zoned out. What if one of those bumps on the ride was me running over someone?
- I could have hit someone. Were there witnesses who have already called the police with my license plate? Am I going to be charged with leaving the scene of an accident?

Pedophilia/ Incest/ Sexual Perversion Obsessions

- Why did I just picture my brother naked?
- Why did I just have a thought of that woman on the street naked? Do I want to rape her? Do I have violent fantasies?
- What if I'm a dark person deep down inside? What if something's wrong with me? What if I'm a pedophile?

Sexual Orientation Obsessions

- What if I'm gay? Am I attracted to my girlfriend/boyfriend enough?
- Why did I look at my same sex friend's lips? Why do I keep doing it? Do I secretly want to kiss him/her?
- (Or conversely, if you are gay) Why did I just look at my opposite sex friend's lips? Why do I keep doing it? Do I secretly want to kiss him/her? I think I'm gay, but what if I'm actually straight?

Negative Thoughts About Oneself

- Whenever I think positive things about myself, that's just me trying to make myself feel better.
- I don't deserve to feel good.

- I'm terrible at everything. I ruin everything.

Fear of Harm Coming to Others
- Why didn't my wife text me back yet?
- Why did I just imagine my son getting in a car accident?
- Whenever I have a bad feeling today. I have to trust it.
- What if I don't do my ritual and someone gets hurt or dies? I'll feel guilty for the rest of my life.

Perfectionism
- I can't ever admit I'm not good at something.
- I should be good at everything as soon as I try it out.
- I have to make the exact best decision.
- Going to therapy means I have "a problem" and I can't admit I have any problems.
- I can't allow myself to think I'm good at anything. That will just lead to complacency.
- I can do this perfectly. And I should be trying to do it perfectly.
- Accepting anything less than perfect is lazy and weak.

Social Obsessions
- Everyone thinks my voice sounds weird. I walk weird.
- That person is mad at me. That person is judging me. That person thinks I did something wrong. That person is yelling at me.
- Why didn't they laugh at my joke? They must all talk about me behind my back. They all think I'm a loser.

Just Right OCD
- I should never leave the house feeling uncomfortable. What if I'm uncomfortable later in the day, during class, and I just can't handle it?
- My mom keeps making a shushing sound that I can't stand. She says she's not doing it, but she does it all the time.
- I need to feel "complete" or "just right." Whenever I feel "not just right" or "incomplete" I need to perform an action to fix the situation and feel "right" and "complete" again.
- Things need to be symmetrical.
- I "need" to do everything an even number of times.

Exit Ramps and Detours (Noticing the Habitual Responses to Your Thoughts and Feelings that Take You Away from Life)

Once you've identified some of the thoughts and feelings that grab your attention, it's time to look at the specific responses (aka rituals) you have to the thoughts that result in you taking that "exit." Let's return to our friend, Jeff. After identifying his triggered thoughts and feelings, he uses the exit ramps to write out the rituals and avoidant behaviors he performs in response to these thoughts and feelings. He notices that the thoughts cause him to get stuck in his head trying to "figure out" if he is a violent person. He will then closely monitor his thoughts, feelings, and behavior in order to try and get answers about his nature and intentions. He also avoids being near sharp objects out of fear that he could use them to stab someone. He writes these behaviors out on the exit ramp.

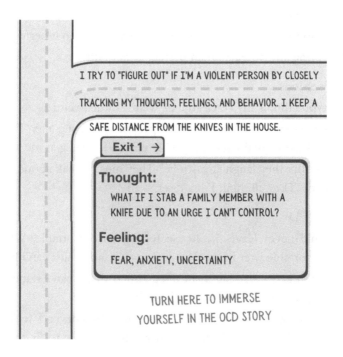

I TRY TO "FIGURE OUT" IF I'M A VIOLENT PERSON BY CLOSELY

TRACKING MY THOUGHTS, FEELINGS, AND BEHAVIOR. I KEEP A

SAFE DISTANCE FROM THE KNIVES IN THE HOUSE.

Exit 1 →

Thought:

WHAT IF I STAB A FAMILY MEMBER WITH A KNIFE DUE TO AN URGE I CAN'T CONTROL?

Feeling:

FEAR, ANXIETY, UNCERTAINTY

TURN HERE TO IMMERSE
YOURSELF IN THE OCD STORY

As you identify your "responses," it's important to be clear about what defines a response. Virtually any behavior that is done with the unwanted thoughts and feelings in mind may constitute a response worth identifying. This includes all behaviors aimed at avoiding, preventing, eliminating, and/or alleviating the impact of the thoughts and feelings on yourself and others. Some of these behaviors will be easy to identify because they are so obviously repetitive, time-consuming, and unproductive. Other behaviors, however, may seem minor and benign, or may be more covert in nature. This second group of behaviors are still important to bring to light because the behaviors are still reinforcing the OCD story as worthy of a response.

For an extensive list of responses that you can have to your thoughts and feelings, be sure to review the lists of compulsions, accommodations, and mental compulsions presented in Chapter 1. But here's a quick list of some of the top contenders for best ways to give your thoughts and feelings your attention:

1. Completing rituals to try and eliminate intrusive thoughts and unwanted feelings. These can include checking, redoing, fixing, and undoing rituals.
2. Ruminating and problem solving in response to your thoughts.
3. Trying to "figure out" if your thoughts are true or not
4. Staying distracted to avoid having to experience intrusive thoughts and unwanted feelings
5. Staying ready and alert for danger and/or bad future events
6. Repetitively reviewing past events
7. Trying to predict / excessively plan for future events
8. Avoiding triggering places, people, or objects
9. Repetitively seeking reassurance from others.
10. Repetitively reassuring yourself

All of these behaviors, believe it or not, amount to giving your unwanted thoughts and feelings your attention. You're reacting to them, and figuring out what to do with them. Even trying to distract yourself, or forcefully keeping your attention focused elsewhere. You are still choosing these behaviors based on the impact they will have on your thoughts and feelings.

On the next page, you'll notice that Jeff has worked through the rest of the worksheet and identified two other "exits" that he is often convinced to take. You can review the completed form on the next page. This is followed by other examples of the OCD Detours worksheet completed by Isabella, a 10-year-old girl struggling with "just right" OCD urges, Darrell, a 20-year-old man who experiences doubts about his memory, Kaley, a 15-year-old girl struggling with perfectionism OCD, and Ali, a 45-year-old woman dealing with fears that she may "go crazy."

You can now go ahead and finish your own OCD Detours worksheet using the 3 exit signs to identify 3 of the OCD patterns you are caught up in. And feel free to complete more than one if that is needed or helpful.

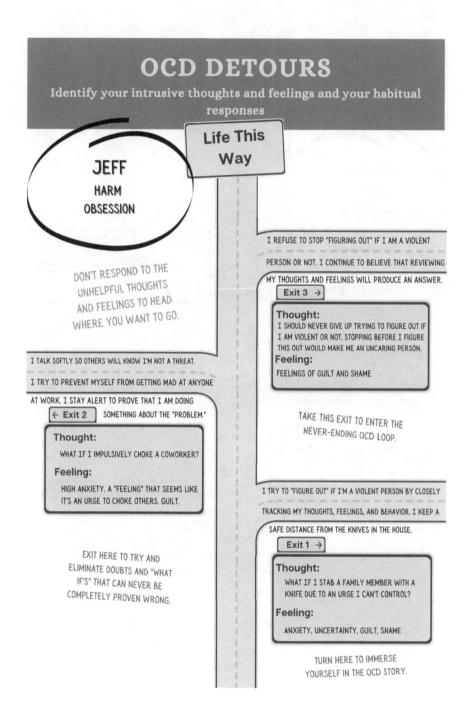

OCD DETOURS

Identify your intrusive thoughts and feelings and your habitual responses

Life This Way

JEFF
HARM
OBSESSION

DON'T RESPOND TO THE UNHELPFUL THOUGHTS AND FEELINGS TO HEAD WHERE YOU WANT TO GO.

I REFUSE TO STOP "FIGURING OUT" IF I AM A VIOLENT PERSON OR NOT. I CONTINUE TO BELIEVE THAT REVIEWING MY THOUGHTS AND FEELINGS WILL PRODUCE AN ANSWER.

← Exit 3 →

Thought:
I SHOULD NEVER GIVE UP TRYING TO FIGURE OUT IF I AM VIOLENT OR NOT. STOPPING BEFORE I FIGURE THIS OUT WOULD MAKE ME AN UNCARING PERSON.

Feeling:
FEELINGS OF GUILT AND SHAME

I TALK SOFTLY SO OTHERS WILL KNOW I'M NOT A THREAT.

I TRY TO PREVENT MYSELF FROM GETTING MAD AT ANYONE

AT WORK. I STAY ALERT TO PROVE THAT I AM DOING

← Exit 2   SOMETHING ABOUT THE "PROBLEM."

Thought:
WHAT IF I IMPULSIVELY CHOKE A COWORKER?

Feeling:
HIGH ANXIETY. A "FEELING" THAT SEEMS LIKE IT'S AN URGE TO CHOKE OTHERS. GUILT.

TAKE THIS EXIT TO ENTER THE NEVER-ENDING OCD LOOP.

I TRY TO "FIGURE OUT" IF I'M A VIOLENT PERSON BY CLOSELY

TRACKING MY THOUGHTS, FEELINGS, AND BEHAVIOR. I KEEP A

SAFE DISTANCE FROM THE KNIVES IN THE HOUSE.

Exit 1 →

Thought:
WHAT IF I STAB A FAMILY MEMBER WITH A KNIFE DUE TO AN URGE I CAN'T CONTROL?

Feeling:
ANXIETY, UNCERTAINTY, GUILT, SHAME

EXIT HERE TO TRY AND ELIMINATE DOUBTS AND "WHAT IF'S" THAT CAN NEVER BE COMPLETELY PROVEN WRONG.

TURN HERE TO IMMERSE YOURSELF IN THE OCD STORY.

85

OCD DETOURS

Identify your intrusive thoughts and feelings and your habitual responses

Life This Way

ISABELLA
"JUST RIGHT"
OBSESSION

DON'T RESPOND TO THE UNHELPFUL THOUGHTS AND FEELINGS TO HEAD WHERE YOU WANT TO GO.

I MAKE MOM REDO MY HAIR UNTIL IF FEELS RIGHT.

I MONITOR MY DAY FOR ANY SIGNS OF A "BAD" DAY.

Exit 3 →

Thought:
IF I DON'T FEEL RIGHT, I WILL HAVE A BAD DAY.

Feeling:
ANXIETY, "NOT RIGHT" FEELING

TAKE THIS EXIT TO ENTER THE NEVER-ENDING OCD LOOP.

IF I DO SOMETHING WITH MY LEFT SIDE, I ALWAYS MAKE SURE I DO THE SAME THING WITH MY RIGHT SIDE.

I NO LONGER PLAY SOCCER TO AVOID TRIGGERS.

← Exit 2

Thought:
WHENEVER I AM ANXIOUS, I NEED TO FIX, OR "EVEN THINGS OUT" TO MAKE IT GO AWAY.

Feeling:
ANXIOUS, FEELING LIKE I AM UNEVEN, A FEAR THAT MY ANXIETY WILL NEVER GO AWAY.

EXIT HERE TO TRY AND ELIMINATE DOUBTS AND "WHAT IF'S" THAT CAN NEVER BE COMPLETELY PROVEN WRONG.

I LIMIT MY CLOTHES TO MY 2 "COMFY" PAIRS OF UNDERWEAR, MY 1 COMFY PAIR OF SOCKS, AND MY 1 COMFY DRESS

I HYPERFOCUS ON MY COMFRORT AND STAY ALERT FOR ANY SIGNS OF DISCOMFORT.

Exit 1 →

Thought:
IF I DON'T CHOOSE THE "RIGHT," CLOTHES, I WILL BE UNCOMFORTABLE AND ANXIOUS ALL DAY.

Feeling:
ANXIOUS, NOT "JUST RIGHT,"

TURN HERE TO IMMERSE YOURSELF IN THE OCD STORY.

OCD DETOURS

Identify your intrusive thoughts and feelings and your habitual responses

Life This Way

DARRELL

FEARS INVOLVING THE RELIABILITY OF HIS MEMORY

I REVIEW LOCAL NEWS FOR STORIES OF SEXUAL ASSAULTS.

I TIRELESSLY REVIEW MY MEMORIES SEEKING CERTAINTY.

DON'T RESPOND TO THE UNHELPFUL THOUGHTS AND FEELINGS TO HEAD WHERE YOU WANT TO GO.

Exit 3 →

Thought:
I BLACKED OUT THE OTHER NIGHT DRINKING WITH FRIENDS. WHAT IF I FORCED MYSELF ON A WOMAN AND DON'T REMEMBER IT?

Feeling:
ANXIETY, UNCERTAINTY, GUILT SHAME, FEAR

I DRIVE HOME MULTIPLE TIMES TO CHECK THE STOVE. I START

TAKING PICTURES OF THE STOVE TURNED OFF EACH MORNING.

TAKE THIS EXIT TO ENTER THE NEVER-ENDING OCD LOOP.

← Exit 2

Thought:
DID I REALLY TURN OFF THE STOVE? I REMEMBER DOING IT BUT MAYBE THAT WAS YESTERDAY.
IMAGES OF MY HOUSE BURNING DOWN.

Feeling:
ANXIETY, UNCERTAINTY

I SEARCH MY MEMORY FOR PROOF AGAINST THE DOUBTS.

I DRIVE BACK HOME LOOKING FOR SIGNS OF AN ACCIDENT.

I CALL MY WIFE ASKING IF SHE THINKS I HIT ANYONE.

Exit 1 →

Thought:
WHAT IF ONE OF THOSE BUMPS I HIT ON THE WAY TO WORK WAS ME HITTING A PERSON AND RUNNING OVER THEM?

Feeling:
ANXIETY, FEAR, GUILT

EXIT HERE TO TRY AND ELIMINATE DOUBTS AND "WHAT IF'S" THAT CAN NEVER BE COMPLETELY PROVEN WRONG.

TURN HERE TO IMMERSE YOURSELF IN THE OCD STORY.

OCD DETOURS

Identify your intrusive thoughts and feelings and your habitual responses

KALEY
PERFECTIONISM
OBSESSION

Life This Way

DON'T RESPOND TO THE UNHELPFUL THOUGHTS AND FEELINGS TO HEAD WHERE YOU WANT TO GO.

I SPEND HOURS STUDYING FOR EVERY LITTLE QUIZ.

I CONSTANTLY REVIEW THE WAYS IN WHICH I COULD BE MORE EFFICIENT AND MORE COMMITTED TO MY WORK.

Exit 3 →

Thought:
I HAVE TO ALWAYS PUT IN THE ABSOLUTE BEST EFFORT.

Feeling:
ANXIETY, GUILT

TAKE THIS EXIT TO ENTER THE NEVER-ENDING OCD LOOP.

I DON'T LET ANYONE MAKE OBSERVATIONS OR STATEMENTS ABOUT ME. I NEVER ADMIT TO OTHERS I HAVE ANY "PROBLEMS."

← Exit 2

Thought:
I NEED TO BE PERFECT. I CAN'T LET OTHERS SEE OR NOTICE MY FLAWS.

Feeling:
ANXIETY, SHAME

EXIT HERE TO TRY AND ELIMINATE DOUBTS AND "WHAT IF'S" THAT CAN NEVER BE COMPLETELY PROVEN WRONG.

I FOCUS ATTENTION ON ANY MISTAKES OR TASKS I CAN'T DO PERFECTLY. I REPETITIVELY "WISH" I WAS BETTER AT THINGS.

Exit 1 →

Thought:
WHY AM I SO MUCH WORSE AT THINGS THAN EVERYONE ELSE?

Feeling:
ANGER, FRUSTRATION, SHAME, ANXIETY

TURN HERE TO IMMERSE YOURSELF IN THE OCD STORY.

OCD DETOURS

Identify your intrusive thoughts and feelings and your habitual responses

Life This Way

ALI

FEAR OF "GOING CRAZY"

DON'T RESPOND TO THE UNHELPFUL THOUGHTS AND FEELINGS TO HEAD WHERE YOU WANT TO GO.

I EXCESSIVELY "PROBLEM SOLVE" HOW TO IMPROVE MY MOOD

IF I NOTICE ANY CHANGES IN MY MOTIVATION OR OUTLOOK.

I TRY TO MAKE SURE I AM "GROUNDED" AND "PRESENT"

AT ALL TIMES.

Exit 3 →

Thought:
I'VE BEEN FEELING BETTER FROM THERAPY. I HAVE TO MAKE SURE I STAY MOTIVATED AND HAPPY.

Feeling:
PRESSURE AND TENSION IN MY HEAD

I STAY ALERT FOR ANY SIGNS OF WORSENING MENTAL HEALTH

I REPETITIVELY REVIEW EVERYTHING I MUST DO ON VACATION

TO MAKE SURE I DON'T "SPIRAL."

← Exit 2

Thought:
WHAT IF MY MENTAL HEALTH SPIRALS AND I RUIN VACATION LIKE I HAVE IN THE PAST?

Feeling:
ANXIETY, SHAME, EMBARRASSMENT

TAKE THIS EXIT TO ENTER THE NEVER-ENDING OCD LOOP.

I CLOSELY MONITOR MY MOTIVATION, MOOD, THINKING ABILITY,

AND TENDENCY TO FOCUS ON MYSELF. I REVIEW MENTAL

HEALTH DIAGNOSES ONLINE OVER AND OVER AGAIN.

Exit 1 →

Thought:
AM I THINKING AS WELL AS I NORMALLY DO? COULD THIS BE A SIGN OF PSYCHOSIS? WHY AM I SO FOCUSED ON MYSELF? AM I A NARCISSIST?

Feeling:
ANXIETY, REDUCED COGNITIVE ABILITY WHEN ANXIOUS

EXIT HERE TO TRY AND ELIMINATE DOUBTS AND "WHAT IF'S" THAT CAN NEVER BE COMPLETELY PROVEN WRONG.

TURN HERE TO IMMERSE YOURSELF IN THE OCD STORY.

You've now created a visual map of your OCD patterns. Let's take a closer look at the various parts of this "map" and see how you might be able to use this information to actually change some of those patterns.

What Does it Actually Mean to Take an Exit?

So what exactly does that exit symbolize? It's essentially where you go when you accept your brain's invitation to explore the intrusive thought. It's a road into your imagination. A place where the intrusive thoughts become convincing and real feeling.

The experiences you have on those exits are likely the reason you're reading this book. These are the parts of your day when you become preoccupied with your obsession, anxious, and uncomfortable, and then turn to mental and physical rituals to alleviate the discomfort.

Taking an exit is an extremely easy thing to do since it can be habitual and almost undetectable. It also often begins with subtle mental activities that you have probably never noticed before, and don't even realize you can control. Your exit occurs the minute you devote your attention to the thoughts and feelings on that exit sign. What this means is that, if you engage in an overt, physical ritual like handwashing, you most likely "take the exit" long before you actually go to the sink to wash your hands. Before doing the overt ritual, you've already asked yourself what invisible germs could have been on the kitchen counter, which resulted in you experiencing a psychosomatic sensation on the fingers that had just touched that surface, which then caused you to visually examine your fingers and the surface of the counter, and debate whether or not you should respond. These earlier mental activities already led you down the exit, and practically guaranteed you would wash your hands. By the time you are washing your hands, you are already far along that exit ramp, deep into your imagination, and far down the OCD rabbit hole.

What Does Passing an Exit Look Like?

The reason why it is important to notice all of the rituals, mental and physical, that lead you down the exit is because you will need to stop all of these behaviors in order to guarantee your success. Even the subtle mental act of trying to "figure out" if you should ritualize or not will usually result in you taking the "exit" and further ritualizing. This is because trying to "figure things out" leads you into your head, and into your imagination. This is the territory of OCD, and this is where OCD will win the argument and convince you to ritualize and/or avoid.

Every exit sign is another alert from your brain, presenting you with information your brain thinks might be important. This is a job that your brain is going to continue to do throughout your day, and throughout your life. And so this skill of passing by the exit is going to be an essential skill in managing your OCD throughout your lifespan. It may seem difficult at first, but once you get the hang of it, you will see that driving by the exits is as easy as committing to the following behavioral changes:

- Not responding to the thoughts
- Not trying to "figure out" if you should respond to your thoughts or feelings
- Not turning to repetitive behaviors to alleviate uncomfortable feelings
- Allowing the thoughts and feelings to enter and exit your awareness in a natural, uncontrolled way
- Not forcefully controlling your attention in an attempt to manage thoughts and feelings
- Letting go of attempts to control your thoughts and feelings
- Letting your guard down / no longer staying alert for danger
- Choosing to think about and do things in the real world because you want to or need to do them, not because these activities are a strategy to "deal with" the thoughts and feelings.

91

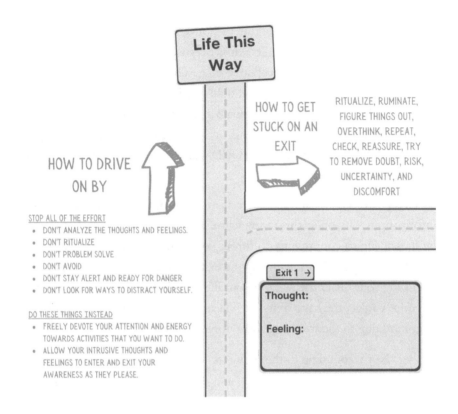

How to Choose to Pass an Exit

As already mentioned, trying to "figure out" whether or not to respond to the thoughts and feelings is a surefire way to end up on an exit. So you're going to have to stop seeing that as the solution. Choosing to pass by an exit is going to have to happen through some other means than trying to out-logic OCD and prove the thoughts to be "false." Here are some of the best ways to find the strength and motivation to pass by the exits.

- No longer reviewing the "content" of your thoughts to decide whether or not they warrant a response. This is a mental ritual. A thought could be scary. It could be possible. It could even seem important. That doesn't mean it makes sense to engage in repetitive mental and physical behaviors every time you have the thought. Instead, simply choose not to respond to any thoughts that trigger your anxiety and make you ritualize. No evaluation of content needed.

- Recognizing that possibilities, "what if's," and "doubts" are, by definition, unable to be disproven. For this reason, focusing on thoughts of this nature, in general, can be a very unproductive way to spend your time and energy.

- Making a commitment before you are triggered. It is sometimes important to commit to stopping your rituals at a time when you are not feeling anxious and triggered. Try deciding which thoughts and feelings you are no longer going to respond to in a calm moment, and eliminating the decision-making process you have been engaging in while triggered.

Exercise: Identify Your Core Fear

Now that you have mapped out some of your current OCD patterns and can see your choices laid out before you, you may still be finding it difficult to take that risk and ignore those OCD "what if's." There is one more piece to the OCD puzzle that should be identified, and it just might provide you with the clarity you need to take those next steps.

Most people with OCD find it helpful to identify what is known as their core fear. This is a fear that is more broad in scope, and deeper, than the specific content of your current obsession. For example, if you are struggling with an obsession that a loved one will die in a car accident, you may be living with a more general fear of being left alone. Your core fear is also the link between your themes if you are experiencing (or have experienced) multiple obsessions. Your obsessive fears that you might be a racist, might not be faithful enough to your boyfriend, and might end up addicted to drugs might all be linked by a core fear "What if there is something morally wrong with me and I will ultimately end up a pariah?" (As you can already see, a great many obsessions can be linked to a core fear of ending up alone in some way). Here are some common core fears. See if any of these resonate with you.

- Being alone
- Lacking value or worth (and ending up alone)
- Being rejected by others
- Being unacceptable
- Letting people down
- Feeling trapped or controlled
- Feeling helpless
- Being a bad person
- Having to experience a specific emotion such as shame or anger indefinitely
- Having to experience anxiety indefinitely
- Causing irreparable harm to yourself or others

Your core fear is the outcome you are ultimately trying to prevent with your rituals and avoidance. It tends to "make sense" in a way that your random obsessional themes do not. For this reason, it can be very illuminating and empowering to put it into words

Identifying your core fear also allows you to face the central motivating force for your OCD behaviors; why you've been avoiding things, why you've been ritualizing. It allows you to see the real issue clearly, and decide how much you actually want this feared outcome to dictate your behavior. After an open evaluation of your fear of "being unacceptable" or "ending up alone," you may decide the actual risk of this occurring is not as great as your behavior has been suggesting. This can increase your willingness 1) to eliminate your rituals, 2) reduce your avoidance, 3) pay less attention to your intrusive thoughts and feelings, and 4) engage in exposures.

One more benefit of identifying your core fear is it prepares you for any new obsessions your OCD might throw at you. Once you understand that you fear "causing irreparable damage to yourself or others," you will be able to face any future obsession OCD throws at you because you'll immediately recognize them as being related to your core fear. You'll be ready for a fear of chemicals. You'll be ready for your obsession around making perfect parenting decisions with your 1-year-old. And you'll be ready for the fear of developing dementia if you don't get enough sleep every night. These new obsessions will always come back to that fear of causing irreparable damage.

As an additional step to help you "avoid the exits," take some time to try and identify your core fear.

1. Review the OCD Detours worksheet and think about your current rituals and avoidance. Ask yourself what you are ultimately trying to avoid. Come up with as many feared outcomes as you can. Exposure to contaminants. Making mistakes. Getting sick. Having something unlucky occur. Whatever it is.

2. Look at these various feared outcomes, and ask yourself "and then what?" with each one. Continue asking this question until you find yourself landing on a final fear that you think might be the core fear. It should look something like this:

    "I'm scared of chemicals"

    "And then what?"

    "They could cause a health problem."

    "And then what?"

    "And I would be responsible for having exposed myself to them. It would be my fault."

    "And then what?"

    "I would have caused irreparable harm to my body and it will be harm that I could have avoided if I'd been smarter and more aware and more responsible.

    "And then what?"

    "I'll feel ashamed and disappointed in myself. And this event will have proven that I'm worthless and inferior."

    "And then what?"

95

"And I'll be exposed to others as someone without value. Others will not want me around because I'm dangerous and irresponsible. That's it. That's as far as the fear goes. That's my core fear."

3. Next make sure that the core fear that you identify links all of your feared outcomes together. There is only ever one core fear, and it should connect with all your obsessive themes.

4. Lastly, take a moment to identify the emotion you would feel if your core fear were to come to pass. You may have already identified feeling an emotion as your core fear. But if you haven't, be sure to notice the feeling you would have to feel as this is probably a key element of your fear.

Going through this process will allow you to clearly see your true feared outcome. The individual with the chemical contamination obsession above now realizes that they need to face their fear of being rejected for being dangerous and irresponsible. If they can start to face that fear, they'll have no problem passing by the exit signs and not getting caught up in the thoughts and feelings related to the chemical obsession. Alternatively, if they had kept the fear at the surface level and just tried to challenge a fear of chemicals, they may have gotten stuck and been unwilling to move forward because they didn't understand the true source of their fear.

Take a moment to complete the worksheet on the next page. Once you've completed it, take a 2nd look at the OCD Detours worksheet and look at the Exit Signs with your core fear in mind. Does being in touch with the core fear clarify why you've been so triggered by these thoughts and feelings. Does it increase your willingness to not give in to those thoughts and feelings? Take note of the core fear you've identified. And keep this in your mind as you continue to work on the exercises in this book. As you think more about your OCD, you may develop more clarity on your core fear. Be sure to fine tune and adjust the core fear you've identified as needed.

Changing the itinerary
Facing Your Core Fear

My greatest (core) fear is:

Additional details, including the outcome I fear and the feelings I would have to feel in that scenario:

The strategies I've been using to prevent this scenario:

Ways I can start to let my guard down:

97

Using Your Own Internal Navigation System (Identifying Where You Want to Go in Life and the "Directions" That Lead You There)

Passing the exits can be easy once you've identified and eliminated all of the behaviors that lead you off course. But sometimes OCD has taken so much away from you that you don't even know what to do with your time if you're not ruminating, worrying, and ritualizing. You're essentially trying to STOP doing something without having a clue as to what you want to START doing instead. Successfully passing those OCD exits may also require you to have other, non-OCD places to go. And these destinations have to come from inside of you (without any interference from OCD).

Looking back at the worksheet you just completed, the question becomes 'What lies on that path ahead once you manage to pass by all of those exits?' What if you could reduce the amount of time you spend responding to your OCD concerns? What if you could forge a path based solely on your values, interests, dreams, life experience, and individual strengths and weaknesses? What if you could set your own coordinates?

When you are struggling with OCD, one of the most important reasons to develop direction is actually quite practical. It's actually a proven scientific fact that the human brain can only focus on one thing at a time, and this has massive ramifications for life with OCD. When you are in the grips of your OCD, any time spend focusing on your obsessions is literally time you are unable to focus on anything else. And the more time you spend thinking about your OCD concerns, the more you lose touch with what's important. And the more you lose touch with what's important, the more space there is in your life to just keep thinking about your obsession. You get the picture. Things can really spiral out of control.

But the opposite is true as well. If you can practice directing your attention towards the things in life that are most important to you - whether that's the activities that bring you meaning or the people you care most about - you're literally unable to focus on your obsessions in those moments. Now this doesn't magically get rid of your upsetting OCD symptoms. Your uncomfortable emotions may continue to be present, and those intrusive thoughts are going to be popping in and out of your awareness. But when you focus on something else in life, the OCD thoughts and feelings can sort of fall into the background. What this means is that identifying alternate targets for your attention is an extremely practical step in managing your OCD symptoms. And this habit can spiral in an opposite, more positive direction. The more time you spend thinking about where you want to go in life, the more personal strengths and interests and relationships you will identify and put effort towards. And the stronger your relationships and personal goals and interests become, the more motivated you will be to put even more time and attention towards those pursuits.

One last point on this. When you are focused on your obsessions, you are focused on what you don't like about life. This can become a lifestyle where you are constantly thinking about the things you want to get away from. Another benefit of identifying "destinations" in life, is that you tap into a whole different way of being. You start to think about the things you like, and the things you want to move towards. It can be a very powerful shift.

The pages ahead will help you identify some of the big important things about you that will be your guide through life, when OCD is not making the decisions. By the end of this section, you'll have identified some very clear behaviors that will help you move closer to what's important in life.

Exercise: Your Travel Journal

It's time to give yourself permission to be in charge of your life again. On the pages that follow, you will be prompted to complete a series of reflective exercises aimed at getting you back in touch with yourself. This is largely a writing exercise, so make sure you have a journal, notebook, or even a laptop handy. But feel free to write your answers in any way that suits your style. You can write out extensive journal entries or lists and bullet points. The main objective is to find the answers that you have inside of you. As you ponder each question, try as hard as you can to respond without your OCD doubts, fears, and urges running the show. And try to keep the perfectionism and the pressures from others out of it. Simply think about your own inner compass, and where you want to go in life. Safe travels!

Destination 1: Core Personal Values (or What Really Matters to You)

Your values are simply the things in life that matter most to you. Identifying your values is all about realizing that there are a lot of important and valuable things in life, but that some things are more important than others. And your opinion about what those things are emerges from your life experience and from the unique perspective you bring as an individual to the world. Knowing your values (and reminding yourself of them) is so important because they guide you in choosing friends, identifying a career, choosing where you want to live, deciding what you do with your free time, and even choosing how you want to carry yourself as a person. They are essential to mapping out your life. So, we're going to practice identifying what values are most important to you at this point in your life. Take a look at the values listed below. The goal of this exercise is to narrow that list down to 5-10 values that represent your most important, personal, core values. Start off by simply crossing out half of the values that don't make the cut. Then continue to cut the remaining values in half as many times as you need until you get down to a list of 5-10 that you feel really represent YOU right now, in this very moment in time. And be sure to not get too hung up on what these words might objectively mean. This exercise is about what these words mean to you.

Achievement	Imagination	Relationships
Adventure	Integrity	Religion
Beauty	Justice	Responsibility
Bravery	Kindness	Risk
Challenge	Knowledge	Safety
Comfort	Leadership	Service
Community	Learning	Skill
Creativity	Love	Spirituality
Curiosity	Meaning	Stability
Empathy	Morality	Status
Exploration	Mindfulness	Strength
Faith	Optimism	Success
Family	Organization	Sustainability
Fame	Passion	Tradition
Flexibility	Peace	Teamwork
Freedom	Personal Growth	Trust
Generosity	Power	Wealth
Health	Reason	Wisdom
Humor	Recreation	

1. List the 5-10 core values you've identified:

2. Describe any recent moments when you were able to make decisions based on some of your core values, even when OCD may have wanted you to make a different decision.

3. Did it feel uncomfortable or unusual to live this way?

4. Did you experience any benefits from living this way?

5. Can you identify the specific behaviors you performed that led you to feel aligned with those values?

Destination 2: Personal Experiences

When you have OCD, you doubt yourself. In fact, it can be outright difficult to trust yourself at all. This leads you to become dependent on external sources for guidance. Things like reassurance from others and looking for answers online become your go-to strategies for dealing with the constant doubts. It's therefore critically important to practice trusting yourself, and that starts with trusting your own experience. Looking into your past experiences and identifying what you've thought and felt in response to the world. For this exercise, you're going to take some time to identify some of the important high points in your life. If you've been struggling with OCD for your entire life, or have had other major challenges in life, this may actually be a difficult question to answer. That's okay. Take your time. Those high points are there if you look closely enough. And they don't have to involve you graduating Cum Laude, surrounded by your devoted followers. They can be things like an afternoon you spent with someone special or a class that you really enjoyed. Whatever it was that brought you to feel your best.

1. What have been the best moments in your life?

2. What were the specific details of these moments that most impacted you? The location? The people you were with? The activity you were engaged in?

3. What events led up to you experiencing this moment?

4. Have you noticed any recent moments where you were able to experience a hint of that feeling? Be sure to think hard about this one. It could be as simple as a single activity or event or conversation. No matter how small, this is really important information for helping you find a direction for yourself.

5. What OCD habits or behaviors are the biggest barrier to you having more of these moments?

6. What steps can you take to increase the chance that you will have more of these experiences in the present?

Destination 3: Family and Friends

Introvert or extrovert. It doesn't matter. Human beings are social creatures. Our relationships can be a major source of happiness in life. When OCD interferes with your relationships, it takes that away from you. And not having those strong social supports can make you even more anxious and depressed. Take some time to consider the people who are important to you, the state of your current relationships, and if you see any path towards becoming closer to these friends and family members.

1. Who are the people most important to you?

2. What do you most appreciate about these relationships?

3. Describe the person you want to be in your relationships with those important to you.

4. Identify 1-3 recent moments when you felt close to one or more of the important people in your life. What were you doing? What was the other person doing? What led up to this moment happening?

5. Which OCD habits and behaviors are the biggest barrier to you feeling closer to your friends and family?

6. Can you think of any behaviors that you can take to increase the number of moments when you feel closer to the important people in your life?

Destination 4: Work, School, and Career

Many people will spend more time at their job than anywhere else. And that doesn't have to be a bad thing. Pursuing a career, or if you're really lucky, a calling, infuses your life with meaning, purpose, and direction. And it can be another positive area of your life to focus your attention. Consider the following questions and do your best to keep the external expectations and the perfectionism out of it. This is just about knowing yourself and allowing that to form your path.

1. When have you felt the most sense of purpose in your life? What sort of work or service were you doing? Were you part of a team? Or working alone? Were you following instructions from someone else? Or were you in charge of your work? Were the hours you worked part of what made it a positive experience?

2. Is this work something that is replicable in your current life (if you're not currently doing it)? Is it something you can find a way to create for yourself moving forward?

3. What do you think are your greatest skills (i.e., what are you good at)?

4. What have others told you are your strengths?

5. Do you have any challenges, preferences, and/or weaknesses that would help you identify jobs/careers that are not good for you?

6. Do you have any academic or career goals for yourself currently?

7. Have you noticed any OCD symptoms that are currently preventing you from pursuing those goals?

8. Do you have any opportunities in your present life situation to take steps towards achieving those goals? Are there small steps you can take to accomplish this on a daily basis?

Destination 5: Free Time

Lastly, let's look at the hours between work and family. Finding good hobbies, interests, and pastimes is essential to a happy life, but OCD can sometimes interfere with this. Your preferred pastimes might be quiet and solitary (prime conditions for obsessing and worrying). Or you might be so busy ritualizing that you are simply forgetting to devote time to your interests. OCD might even be telling you that you can't waste any time or do anything inefficiently (i.e., do things for fun). It's time for you to embrace what you enjoy doing and set some goals for yourself in this area. The longer the list of distracting, engaging, fulfilling, and meaningful activities that you have at your disposal, the more you are going to be setting yourself up for success.

1. What hobbies and pastimes bring you the most joy and/or satisfaction?

2. Have there been any moments lately when you did something new in your leisure time that you truly enjoyed?

3. Do you have any goals for yourself that you would like to pursue in your free time?

4. What free time activities are most important to you right now at this point in time?

5. Are there any OCD symptoms that are stopping you from doing these activities that are important to you?

6. Have you noticed any recent steps you've taken that allowed you to spend more time enjoying these activities.

105

Exercise: The Set Your Destination Worksheet

Flip forward to find the Set Your Destination worksheet. Go ahead and fill in the 3 OCD Exit Signs and Exit Ramps based on what you wrote on the OCD Detours worksheet. Now turn your attention to the new "Destinations" sections at the top of the worksheet. Now that you've done some thinking about the things that matter most, you're going to home in on two destinations you'd like to be moving towards. These might be things you've been neglecting because of your OCD, or things that you're simply ready to start paying more attention to. You can choose people, activities, career goals, or any other part of your life that you'd like to move towards.

Take a moment to appreciate the two destinations you've identified. These are destinations that come from YOU, not your OCD. You are now using your navigation system to set your coordinates. In this moment you have real destinations, not just things that OCD wants you to get away from.

The next step is just as important as setting your destinations. Look at the "Directions" box on the worksheet. This is where you will identify the specific behaviors that you can take to move closer to those destinations. These could be behaviors you have done in the past, behaviors you are currently doing, or behaviors you've been wanting to start doing. The goal is to identify a list of concrete steps you can take to feel closer to the things that are important to you. These behaviors will go in the "Directions" section.

You may remember our friend Jeff from the OCD Detours worksheet. He's still struggling to stop himself from focusing on intrusive thoughts that he might hurt someone he loves. Jeff finds the strength to momentarily put his fears aside and think about the things in life that are important to him. He identifies 2 priorities to him right now: his wife and his love of cooking.

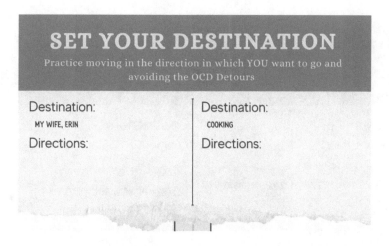

In thinking about recent moments in his life, Jeff then identifies specific behaviors he believes will bring him closer to his wife and his love for cooking. This is important because just identifying what's important doesn't give Jeff any practical guidance. In identifying some behaviors that will take him in the direction of what's important, he knows what action he can take.

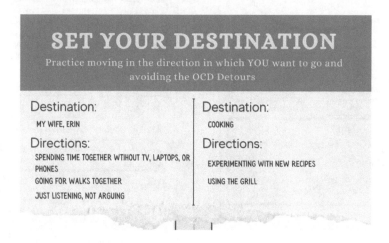

Now it's your turn. Go ahead and complete the worksheet. You can also review 4 examples of the completed form, completed by Jeff, and the 4 other individuals that completed the OCD Detours worksheet earlier in the chapter.

SET YOUR DESTINATION

Practice moving in the direction in which YOU want to go and avoiding the OCD Detours

Destination:

MY WIFE, ERIN

Directions:

SPENDING TIME TOGETHER WTIHOUT TV, LAPTOPS, OR PHONES

GOING FOR WALKS TOGETHER

JUST LISTENING, NOT ARGUING

Destination:

COOKING

Directions:

EXPERIMENTING WITH NEW RECIPES

USING THE GRILL

JEFF
HARM
OBSESSION

I TALK SOFTLY SO OTHERS WILL KNOW I'M NOT A THREAT. I TRY
TO PREVENT MYSELF FROM GETTING MAD AT ANYONE AT WORK.

I STAY ALERT TO PROVE THAT I AM
← Exit 2 | DOING SOMETHING ABOUT THE PROBLEM.

Thought:
WHAT IF I IMPULSIVELY CHOKE A COWORKER?

Feeling:
HIGH ANXIETY. ALSO A FEELING THAT SEEMS
LIKE IT'S AN "URGE" TO CHOKE OTHERS.

I REFUSE TO STOP "FIGURING OUT" IF I AM A VIOLENT

PERSON OR NOT. I CONTINUE TO BELIEVE THAT REVIEWING

MY THOUGHTS AND FEELINGS WILL
Exit 3 → | PRODUCE AN ANSWER.

Thought: I SHOULD NEVER GIVE UP TRYING
TO FIGURE OUT IF I AM VIOLENT OR
NOT. STOPPING BEFORE I FIGURE
Feeling: THIS OUT WOULD MAKE ME AN
FEELING OF FEAR AND UNCARING PERSON.
DREAD

I TRY TO "FIGURE OUT" IF I'M A VIOLENT PERSON BY CLOSELY

TRACKING MY THOUGHTS, FEELINGS, AND BEHAVIOR. I KEEP A

SAFE DISTANCE FROM THE KNIVES IN
Exit 1 → | THE HOUSE.

Thought:
WHAT IF I STAB A FAMILY MEMBER WITH A
KNIFE DUE TO AN URGE I CAN'T CONTROL?
Feeling:
FEAR, ANXIETY, UNCERTAINTY

SET YOUR DESTINATION

Practice moving in the direction in which YOU want to go and avoiding the OCD Detours

Destination:

SOCCER

Directions:

I HAVE TO WEAR SHIN GUARDS.
I HAVE TO LET MY HAIR COME LOOSE DURING PRACTICE.
I CAN FOCUS ON IMPROVING MY PASSING AND SHOOTING AND LETTING MYSELF BE "OFF KILTER."
I CAN INVITE FRIENDS OUT FOR PIZZA AFTER GAMES.

Destination:

MY RELATIONSHIP WITH MY MOM

Directions:

I CAN TALK MORE PATIENTLY WITH MOM WHEN OCD IS BAD.
MOM AND I CAN SET A LIMIT TO THE NUMBER OF HAIR "REDOS" IN THE MORNING.
MOM AND I CAN GO CLOTHES SHOPPING TOGETHER AT THE MALL.

ISABELLA
"JUST RIGHT"
OBSESSION

IF I DO SOMETHING WITH MY LEFT SIDE, I ALWAYS MAKE SURE I DO THE SAME THING WITH MY RIGHT SIDE.

I NO LONGER PLAY SOCCER TO AVOID TRIGGERS.

← Exit 2

Thought:
WHENEVER I AM ANXIOUS, I NEED TO FIX, OR "EVEN THINGS OUT" TO MAKE IT GO AWAY.
Feeling:
ANXIOUS, FEELING LIKE I AM UNEVEN, A FEAR THAT MY ANXIETY WILL NEVER GO AWAY

I MAKE MOM REDO MY HAIR UNTIL IF FEELS RIGHT.

THIS SOMETIMES TAKES 10-20 TRIES.

Exit 3 →

Thought:
IF I DON'T FEEL RIGHT, I WILL HAVE A BAD DAY.
Feeling:
ANXIETY, "NOT RIGHT" FEELING

I LIMIT MY CLOTHES TO MY 2 "COMFY" PAIRS OF UNDERWEAR,

MY 1 COMFY PAIR OF SOCKS, AND MY 1 COMFY DRESS.

Exit 1 →

Thought:
IF I DON'T CHOOSE THE "RIGHT," CLOTHES, I WILL BE UNCOMFORTABLE AND ANXIOUS ALL DAY.
Feeling:
ANXIOUS, NOT "JUST RIGHT,"

SET YOUR DESTINATION

Practice moving in the direction in which YOU want to go and avoiding the OCD Detours

Destination:
FRIENDS

Directions:
I CAN HAVE DRINKS WITH MY FRIEND AT OUR FAVORITE BAR AND FOCUS ON ENJOYING HIS COMPANY.

I CAN INVITE MY FEMALE FRIEND TO MY HOUSE TO PLAY VIDEO GAMES.

I CAN FOCUS BEING ON TIME TO PLANS AND NOT RETRACING MY ROUTES.

Destination:
MY ART

Directions:
I CAN SET ASIDE TIME TO GO TO THE ART SUPPLIES STORE.

I CAN GET BACK INTO MY GRAFFITI ART ON CANVAS.

I CAN SET UP AN ETSY ACCOUNT TO START SELLING MY WORK.

DARRELL

FEARS INVOLVING THE RELIABILITY OF HIS MEMORY

I REVIEW LOCAL NEWS FOR STORIES OF SEXUAL ASSAULTS.

I TIRELESSLY REVIEW MY MEMORIES SEEKING CERTAINTY.

Exit 3 →

Thought:
I BLACKED OUT THE OTHER NIGHT DRINKING WITH FRIENDS. WHAT IF I FORCED MYSELF ON A WOMAN AND DON'T REMEMBER IT?

Feeling:
ANXIETY, UNCERTAINTY, GUILT SHAME, FEAR

I DRIVE HOME MULTIPLE TIMES TO CHECK THE STOVE. I START TAKING PICTURES OF THE STOVE TURNED OFF EACH MORNING.

I SEARCH MY MEMORY FOR PROOF AGAINST THE DOUBTS.

I DRIVE BACK HOME LOOKING FOR SIGNS OF AN ACCIDENT.

← Exit 2

Thought:
DID I REALLY TURN OFF THE STOVE? I REMEMBER DOING IT BUT MAYBE THAT WAS YESTERDAY. I SEE IMAGES OF MY HOUSE BURNING DOWN.

Feeling:
ANXIETY, UNCERTAINTY

I CALL MY WIFE ASKING IF SHE THINKS I HIT ANYONE.

Exit 1 →

Thought:
WHAT IF ONE OF THOSE BUMPS I HIT ON THE WAY TO WORK WAS ME HITTING A PERSON AND RUNNING OVER THEM?

Feeling:
ANXIETY, FEAR, GUILT

SET YOUR DESTINATION

Practice moving in the direction in which YOU want to go and avoiding the OCD Detours

Destination:
FRIENDS

Directions:

I INVITE MY BEST FRIEND TO A CONCERT.
I START A BRACELET-MAKING CLUB AT SCHOOL (AFTER IDENTIFYING THAT MAKING BRACELETS IS AN ACTIVITY THAT DOESN'T TRIGGER MY OCD).
I WEAR A BRACELET THAT HAS A MISTAKE ON IT AND SHOW IT TO FRIENDS.

Destination:
NATURE

Directions:

I START GOING FOR MORE HIKES WITH MY FAMILY.
I START A GARDEN IN THE BACKYARD.
I LET "MOTHER NATURE" DECIDE HOW WELL MY VEGETABLES WILL DO.
I ACCEPT THAT I CAN "GRADUALLY GET BETTER" AT GARDENING.

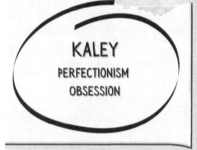

KALEY

PERFECTIONISM
OBSESSION

I DON'T LET ANYONE MAKE OBSERVATIONS OR STATEMENTS

ABOUT ME. I NEVER ADMIT TO OTHERS I HAVE ANY "PROBLEMS."

← Exit 2

Thought:
I NEED TO BE PERFECT. I CAN'T LET OTHERS SEE OR NOTICE MY FLAWS.

Feeling:
ANXIETY, SHAME

I SPEND HOURS STUDYING FOR EVERY LITTLE QUIZ.

I CONSTANTLY REVIEW THE WAYS IN WHICH I COULD BE

MORE EFFICIENT AND MORE COMMITTED TO MY WORK.

Exit 3 →

Thought:
I HAVE TO ALWAYS PUT IN THE ABSOLUTE BEST EFFORT.

Feeling:
ANXIETY, GUILT

I FOCUS ATTENTION ON ANY MISTAKES OR TASKS I CAN'T DO

PERFECTLY. I REPETITIVELY "WISH" I WAS BETTER AT THINGS.

Exit 1 →

Thought:
WHY AM I SO MUCH WORSE AT THINGS THAN EVERYONE ELSE?

Feeling:
ANGER, FRUSTRATION, SHAME, ANXIETY

SET YOUR DESTINATION

Practice moving in the direction in which YOU want to go and avoiding the OCD Detours

Destination:

GO ON VACATION WITH MY FAMILY

Directions:

MAKE VACATION PLANS AS A FAMILY
ENJOY THE BEACH
REMAIN FLEXIBLE ABOUT THE DAILY SCHEDULE
ALLOW MYSELF TO NOT BE IN A PERFECT MOOD
AVOID RUMINATING ABOUT BAD MEMORIES FROM PAST
VACATIONS

Destination:

MY RELATIONSHIP WITH MY SON

Directions:

I CAN CATCH MY SON BEING GOOD AND GIVE HIM MORE
POSITIVE FEEDBACK.
I CAN TAKE MY SON AND ANOTHER FRIEND OUT FOR A FUN
ACTIVITY (AND RESIST RUMINATING IN THE PROCESS).

ALI
FEAR OF "GOING CRAZY"

I EXCESSIVELY "PROBLEM SOLVE" HOW TO IMPROVE MY MOOD
IF I NOTICE ANY CHANGES IN MY MOTIVATION OR OUTLOOK.

I TRY TO MAKE SURE I AM "GROUNDED"
AND "PRESENT" AT ALL TIMES.

Exit 3 →

Thought:
I'VE BEEN FEELING BETTER FROM THERAPY.
I HAVE TO MAKE SURE I STAY MOTIVATED
AND HAPPY.
Feeling:
PRESSURE AND TENSION IN MY HEAD

I STAY ALERT FOR ANY SIGNS OF WORSENING MENTAL HEALTH

I REPETITIVELY REVIEW EVERYTHING I MUST DO ON VACATION

← Exit 2 TO MAKE SURE I DON'T "SPIRAL."

Thought:
WHAT IF MY MENTAL HEALTH SPIRALS AND I
RUIN VACATION LIKE I HAVE IN THE PAST?
Feeling:
ANXIETY, SHAME, EMBARRASSMENT

I CLOSELY MONITOR MY MOTIVATION, MOOD, THINKING ABILITY,

AND TENDENCY TO FOCUS ON MYSELF. I REVIEW MENTAL

HEALTH DIAGNOSES ONLINE
Exit 1 → OVER AND OVER AGAIN.

Thought:
AM I THINKING AS WELL AS I NORMALLY DO?
COULD THIS BE A SIGN OF PSYCHOSIS? WHY AM I
SO FOCUSED ON MYSELF? AM I A NARCISSIST?
Feeling:
ANXIETY, REDUCED COGNITIVE ABILITY WHEN
ANXIOUS

SET YOUR DESTINATION

Practice moving in the direction in which YOU want to go and avoiding the OCD Detours

Destination:

Destination:

Directions:

Directions:

Exit 3 →

Thought:

Feeling:

← Exit 2

Thought:

Feeling:

Exit 1 →

Thought:

Feeling:

Available for download at *https://pittsburghocdtreatment.com/publications/the-ocd-travel-guide/*

Once you've completed the worksheet, you now have the opportunities to make some observations and draw some conclusions.

- First, notice how the **Exit Signs** contain the thoughts and feelings you want to get away from, while the **Destinations** contain the things in life you would like to get closer to. Ask yourself how much of your recent thinking has been consumed by the Exit Signs vs. focused on your Destinations.

- Second, notice how the **Exit Ramps** contain the actions you take to try and get rid of the thoughts and feelings you don't like, while the **Directions** contain the actions you can take to get closer to what matters. Consider how much of your time is spent engaging in the behavior on the Exit Ramps vs. engaging in the behavior in the Directions.

- In general, how much time are you spending on those exit ramps vs driving towards your destinations? How much time are you trying to get away from things you don't like and how much time are you moving towards what you like? Take note of any imbalances you see that you are not happy with. Allow these imbalances to enter into your awareness. See if they provide you with any clarity or increased motivation.

- Realize that you can start to work on the imbalance whenever you'd like. It really is as simple as spending more time engaging in the behaviors that bring you closer to what you like and, as a consequence, spending less time completing rituals and avoidance in response to the thoughts and feelings you don't like.

Focusing on What's Important vs. Avoiding OCD Thoughts and Feelings

So, you might be a little confused about the difference between directing your attention towards what's important in life and engaging in avoidant behavior that worsens your OCD. The key here is that there is a right way and a wrong way to focus on something else.

Let's start with the wrong way: If you are purposefully trying to eliminate intrusive thoughts and get rid of your uncomfortable emotions, then you are engaging in a ritual or other avoidant behavior. For example, thinking positive thoughts so that you can eliminate, undo, or fix negative thoughts is a ritual. That is not an example of focusing on what's important. Properly focusing on what's important is not going to eliminate your unwanted thoughts and feelings. And that shouldn't be the goal.

Now, for the right way: When you are focused on what's important in a helpful way, you don't argue with, disprove, or attempt to negate your OCD thoughts. You don't try to eliminate your emotions. You don't complete rituals before, during, or after the time you are focusing on other things. You simply focus on what's important no matter what OCD thoughts and feelings you are experiencing. And you also don't expect your thoughts and feelings to go away just because you're focusing on something else. You actually choose to live with your uncomfortable thoughts and emotions.

Keep in mind that there is not always an obvious, immediate benefit to this strategy. It might not feel good to focus on something else when you are having uncomfortable thoughts and feelings. At least not at first. But once you start this habit and get better at focusing on where you want to go, fill your life up with more of the good stuff, and spend less time thinking about what you want to get away from, you are taking the first step towards breaking free from the Cycle of Avoidance.

Chapter 4

START Your Journey (Strategies for Venturing Out onto the Open Road and Living with Unwanted Thoughts and Feelings)

When you start to put your plan from Chapter 3 into action and begin moving in the direction of what's important, you are setting the stage for a whole host of natural exposures. With the example of Jeff from Chapter 3 who is struggling with the harm obsessions, the more he moves towards his goal of cooking, the more he will have to use sharp objects, and be near other people while using those sharp objects, and the more his fear, anxiety, and disturbing thoughts are going to increase. He's going to need some help if he's to successfully stick with his plan to cook, and not go back to ritualizing and avoiding.

Luckily for Jeff, and for anyone struggling with OCD, there are some proven approaches for successfully navigating the exposures that life throws at you. In this chapter, we're going to look at a simple, easy to remember approach that you can use to go anywhere you want to go in life, while managing OCD in the process. It's called the START method, as in 'start' to take your life back from OCD, and it consists of 5 steps. This chapter will detail those 5 steps, as well as provide a host of strategies to help you in following this method.

START

To Take Your Life Back From OCD

Step 1	**S**ET YOUR DESTINATION
Step 2	**T**AKE STEPS TOWARDS YOUR GOAL
Step 3	**A**CKNOWLEDGE THOUGHTS AND FEELINGS
Step 4	**R**EFOCUS ON YOUR GOAL
Step 5	**T**OLERATE DISCOMFORT

Available for download at *https://pittsburghocdtreatment.com/publications/the-ocd-travel-guide/*

Step 1 SET YOUR DESTINATION

The first step is something we've already explored in depth, but be careful not to downplay how important, and how difficult, this step can be. It starts with asking yourself some questions that OCD often doesn't want you to ask. When your life doesn't revolve around the intrusive thoughts, the rules, the fears, and the doubts, where is it YOU want to go? What is OCD stopping you from doing? What do you want to do with your day today? What do you want to do with the next hour? What do you want to do at this very moment?

Answering any of these questions may cause you to enter into a natural exposure, because OCD doesn't like it when you think about what YOU want to do. This may cause anxiety. This may feel unsafe. But that's okay. Give yourself permission to identify what you want to do without fear, and without questioning yourself. It might be something as simple as playing a video game, going for a walk, or watching a movie. Give yourself permission to do what you want to do. And then put it into words. You can say it out loud or just in your head:

"I am going to wear my favorite t-shirt, which I haven't been able to wear in years."

"I am going to attend that job interview."

"I am going to drive to my brother's house for my niece's birthday party."

Another very important consideration during this step is that you want to take care in identifying destinations that are NOT OCD goals or perfectionistic goals. Be careful not to create any of the following destinations:

- Destinations that involve perfecting your rituals

- Destinations that involve improving your avoidance

- Destinations that involve unattainable or perfectionistic goals

- Destinations that involve achieving certainty or eliminating risk

In order to avoid these pitfalls, you may have to set destinations for yourself that you're not used to setting. They may seem unexciting or disappointing in relation to the usual goals you set for yourself. You may, for example, have to set a destination for yourself like "I'm going to cook an adequate dinner for the family" instead of "I'm going to cook this recipe perfectly and be as efficient with my time as I possibly can in the process." The new destination you are setting for yourself might seem a little boring, but it's going to be realistic and, more importantly, achievable. The OCD goals you usually set for yourself, on the other hand, may seem more enticing but are unachievable and only lead to frustration and wasted time. Setting this new goal for yourself is truly about taking your life back from OCD.

Step 2 — TAKE STEPS TOWARDS YOUR GOAL

This next step is very straightforward. Now that you've set a destination, you simply have to move in that direction. Just like Step 1, this step may be an exposure to some degree. If your OCD likes to make you wait, and plan, and predict, and then wait some more, this step will require you to move before you feel ready. And this may be a whole new mindset to practice; simply moving before thoroughly and excessively thinking things through. In order to make this happen, take a brief moment to identify the initial steps you can take towards your goal, and then start taking those steps as soon as possible. So, if the goal you set for yourself in Step 1 is to be able to eat leftover meals, step 2 will simply involve taking a series of steps including 1)

119

walking to the refrigerator, 2) retrieving leftovers, 3) heating them up, and 4) eating them. If your goal is to socialize more with friends, Step 2 will involve actually calling or texting a friend to ask them if they would like to hang out.

Step 2 is all about putting an end to the thinking. It's about moving and living and experiencing. So, go ahead and take those first steps!

Step 3 — ACKNOWLEDGE THOUGHTS AND FEELINGS

Once you've taken those first steps towards your goal, the intrusive thoughts and uncomfortable feelings have most likely already begun. It's important that you don't try and act like the thoughts and feelings aren't happening. That would just amount to avoidance. On the contrary, you're going to want to acknowledge their presence. This is your first step towards choosing exposure over avoidance. And it's how you'll be showing OCD that you're not afraid. The thoughts and feelings are happening. That's okay. And you can handle it. And don't worry if you feel like you're in a 'fake it 'til you make it' situation. That's often the case when you first start facing your OCD fears. During this step, there are a number of important things you can do to acknowledge your thoughts and feelings in a helpful and productive way. These approaches all help you to accept the fact that you are having these thoughts and feelings, while also creating some healthy distance between YOU and YOUR THOUGHTS. In the process, you're allowing yourself to have thoughts you don't necessarily agree with or find helpful, and have feelings you don't like all that much.

As you acknowledge your thoughts and feelings, keep in mind that the overarching goal is to allow yourself to have thoughts without getting entangled in the "content." Any thinking that you start to do about the actual words and ideas of your intrusive thoughts will lead you into further into your head, where you are more susceptible to becoming convinced that you must respond to the thoughts.

Below, you'll find a number of different approaches to acknowledging your thoughts and feelings while minimizing your engagement with the content. Be sure to take the time to review these strategies carefully and actually try putting them into practice. This way you can identify the strategies that work best for you.

Strategy — Label Your Intrusive Thoughts and Feelings

How you choose to describe your thoughts and feelings, both to yourself and others, can have a huge impact on how closely you align yourself with those internal experiences that your body is causing you to have. You may be accustomed to describing your intrusive thoughts and feelings in a way that makes them sound like you are choosing to have them, rather than experiences that your body is generating. Consider the following statements that all identify you (the individual) as the source of thoughts and feelings:

"I'm worried if I wear my favorite shirt, something bad will happen to me today."

"I'm scared that the person at the job interview will think I'm an idiot."

"I'm scared I will have a panic attack driving through the tunnels to get to my brother's house."

"I'm so anxious."

The problem with statements like these is that they can leave you feeling stuck, and unable to identify what you can do to change anything. They are also inaccurate descriptions of how thoughts and feelings actually work. In truth, your intrusive thoughts are simply the result of your brain's efforts to

121

warn you of *possible* danger. Your feelings, meanwhile, are the product of complex neurobiological processes that are largely outside of your control. Recognizing that you can't control your intrusive thoughts and feelings is essential. It allows you to focus on what you can control, which is whether or not you respond to those thoughts and feelings. Instead of the above statements, try acknowledging your thoughts and feelings in the following, more accurate, manner:

- Instead of saying, "I'm worried if I wear my favorite shirt, something bad will happen to me today."

  Try saying to yourself, "The thought popped into my head that something bad will happen to me if I wear my favorite shirt."

- Instead of saying, "I'm scared that the person at the job interview is going to think I'm an idiot."

  Try saying to yourself, "I just noticed my brain having the thought 'The person at the job interview s going to think I'm an idiot.'"

- Instead of saying, "I'm scared I will have a panic attack driving through the tunnels to get to my brother's house."

  Try saying to yourself, "My brain is telling me I'm going to have a panic attack if I drive through any tunnels today."

- And rather than saying "I'm so anxious."

  Try saying to yourself, "My body is having an anxious sensation."

The beauty of describing your thoughts and feelings in this way is that it opens you up to a world of possibility. Your thoughts and feelings are now accurately attributed to your brain, and now you get to decide how you respond to the thought. You can choose if you want the thought to be important or not, and whether or not you want to give the thought power.

Strategy Give the Internal Experiences a Name

Overcoming OCD requires that you detach your thoughts and feelings from the value and meaning you have been giving them. One of the strategies that can help to empty your OCD experiences of charged meaning is to come up with names for your various OCD symptoms. For example, you can identify a name for these random, repetitive, intrusive thoughts your OCD makes you experience. Good names will emphasize their lack of significance. Here are a few you can try to use. Or come up with your own.

- Intrusive Thoughts

- "What if's" or Possibilities

- Detours

- Worry Thoughts

- Worry Tricks

- Junk Thoughts

- Brain Hiccups

Just as you want to separate yourself from thoughts, you want to do the same thing with OCD-triggered feelings. The emotional responses you have to the world are just as likely as your thoughts to be unhelpful signals not deserving of your attention. Your anxiety, for example, can be functioning very much like a broken smoke alarm, which happens to be a great name to give your OCD feelings. Here are some other ideas:

- The Anxious Sensation

- The False Alarm

- The Angry Feeling

123

- The Guilty Feeling

- The Grossed Out Feeling

- The Lizard Brain

Good names can delegitimize the thoughts and feelings and make them easier to ignore. They can remind you of the repetitive, inconsequential nature of these internal experiences.

Strategy — Thank OCD (or Thank Your Brain)

Another strategy that can really emphasize the difference between you and your thoughts is to practice the strategy of "thanking your brain" or "thanking OCD." This skill is as simple as it sounds. Whenever you are having thoughts that trigger you, you can literally thank your brain for the thoughts. Taking the above thoughts as an example, this might look something like this:

- "Thank you brain for giving me the thought 'Something bad will happen if I wear my favorite shirt.'"

- "Thank you OCD for giving me the thought 'The person at the job interview is going to think I'm an idiot.'"

- "Thank you brain for giving me the thought 'I'll have a panic attack if I go through any tunnels today.'"

If it helps you can even throw in an extra word to describe the thought like "silly," "ridiculous," and "goofy." By creating this conversation between you and your brain or you and your OCD, you are emphasizing that your brain and/or your OCD is causing the thought to occur, and that you have the choice in how you respond to the thought.

Strategy   Acknowledge Your Core Fear

Chapter 3 introduced the idea of the core fear. If you haven't yet completed the activity, Changing Your Itinerary, you may want to do that now. As you allow the intrusive thoughts and feelings to exist while not responding with mental rituals, you may find it helpful to reflect on the core fear that is at the root of these thoughts. Saying to yourself, "there's my fear of ending up all alone." or "there is my fear of being controlled showing up again" can help you get right to the heart of the matter. This approach can also help you to acknowledging the presence of your triggered inner experience without getting entangled in the messy details of the specific thing OCD wants you to worry about. Try coming up with a statement that reminds you of your core fear but also addresses it in a relaxed manner.

- There's my fear that "I'll be rejected by others."
- There's the "people will think I'm worthless" fear.
- Here's my fear of "the feeling of being left."
- I'm noticing my "I'll let everyone down" fear.
- Looks like the fear "I'm going to be trapped" stopped by.
- My fear of "feeling shame" is showing up again.

Once you've reminded yourself of your core fear, it's time to change your response to this fear. If you let your core fear win, you'll inevitably recoil and return to avoidance. Decide if you're ready to stop protecting yourself from your fear and find out what happens. Maybe nothing will happen. Maybe someday that feared scenario might happen. And yet, will it have been worth it to be living your life differently? Be sure to pay particular attention to the

125

emotion you are trying to avoid. That is usually what all of the avoidance is about. What if you do let your guard down and have to feel what it feels like to be left or rejected? Maybe it's time to let yourself be vulnerable to letting this happen. Maybe you could handle the feeling. Maybe it's worth the risk.

Strategy — Add Context to the Reductive OCD Story

Of all of the strategies, this one runs the greatest risk of getting you caught up in the content of your thoughts, and ritualizing. So make sure to employ this one carefully, and avoid getting into an argument with your thoughts. You are "adding" to the OCD story in your head, not trying to argue with it, negate it, or prove it wrong.

OCD loves to oversimplify everything. It doesn't like nuance. It doesn't like complexity. And it definitely doesn't like the gray areas of life. What does OCD say is happening every time you hear laughter in the hallway in school or at work? Well, those people are all making fun of you of course! Why is it you sometimes make mistakes and don't get things the first time? Well, obviously it's because you're awful at everything you put your mind to.

When OCD is constantly making you fear the worst, you can grow so weary of battling the negative thoughts that you eventually allow the negative story to become THE story. It's just easier than trying to constantly proving the thoughts wrong. You start to internalize the story as if it were absolute fact. Over time, you forget that you didn't initially agree with the OCD story and made an effort to counter it. That story in your head can make you feel bad in a fairly permanent way. Here are some examples of black and white, reductive OCD thoughts that can get stuck in your thinking over time.

- I'm mean or rude.

- People don't like me.

- I'm a bad person.

- I can't handle things.

- I'm bad at things.

- I'm untrustworthy.

- I'm lazy.

- People will reject me.

Not exactly a fun group of thoughts to have stuck in your head, but for so many with OCD, these are the stories they are walking around with. Let's look at a few things that you can do to start to soften, and expand the overly simplistic, negative, and twisted worldview that OCD wants you to believe.

Allow multiple "what if's" into your awareness and embrace the uncertainty: Sure, those people could be laughing at you. But they could also be laughing at something else entirely. You simply don't have information one way or the other so don't follow that OCD urge that you have to settle on one of the two options, and draw a conclusion. Allow yourself to generate more "what if" possibilities, including some positive outcomes. Allow yourself to not know the truth. Ironically, that's where the actual truth lies.

Think about yourself and the world fully: Don't forget that a solitary word, judgment, or label can never capture all of you or completely explain any situation. You've had people that have rejected you in small and big ways, but you've had people who have truly seen you as the apple of their eye. You've made lots of mistakes in life, but you've had lots of achievements, both big and small. Resist simplistic explanations. You are a complicated, irreducible human who can never be reduced to a stereotype.

Don't forget that there are multiple reasons for why things happen: So, you went through a messy divorce? And OCD wants you to think this is just another reason to blame yourself, and only yourself, for everything that didn't work out. You have to start being more fair minded with yourself. Don't forget that others are not perfect and are partly responsible for outcomes in your life. Don't forget that there are things beyond your control, in the world

127

around you, having an impact on things. You've had your own unique upbringing, your own unique history, and are immersed in a unique present context, including your current school/work situation, your current friends and acquaintances, and current physical location. All of these variables are playing a part. So, look at more causes than just YOU. Look at more explanations. Allow yourself to really understand why things have happened.

Appropriately blame OCD when it's warranted: Maybe some things haven't gone your way. Maybe you have struggled with relationships. Maybe you have had trouble in school. Maybe things with your career haven't always gone smoothly. Don't forget all of the things that can be explained by having OCD. OCD can make it difficult to concentrate. It can make it difficult to maintain relationships. And it can make you behave in ways that aren't really the way you would behave if given the chance to fully direct your actions. OCD deserves some major blame for a lot of the negative things that have occurred in your life. This is an across-the-board fact for everyone struggling with this diagnosis.

Be ready for the OCD backlash: Naturally, you can expect OCD to have a response once you start trying to add some context and nuance to your story. OCD generally likes to double down with even more reductionist thoughts. Don't be surprised to hear OCD saying "You're just being lazy. You're just making excuses. Face the facts. It really is your fault." And you can simply go ahead and label these responses as more of OCD's sad attempts to create that un-nuanced, oversimplified, reductive story about what is going on.

Strategy Stop the Argument in Your Head. Agree with the Possibility.

"What if you are secretly a violent person who is going to kill someone in the future?"

"What if you are going to hell?"

"What if you have cancer?"

"What if you don't really know yourself?"

"What if you are going to lose your mind in the future?"

"What if that dust on the counter is lead dust?"

"What if you are racist?"

"What if you don't really love your partner?"

These are all examples of intrusive thoughts. When you don't like the intrusive thoughts you are experiencing, you start to do all you can to silence them. You embark on an endless search for that one argument, or that one piece of evidence, that will prove the thought wrong. Maybe you're hoping that if you think about the situation long enough, you'll eventually figure out the truth. Or maybe you're hoping that if you do enough checks, and enough rituals, the thoughts will just stop. But these efforts are all ultimately attempts to achieve the impossible. If you take a look at that list of intrusive thoughts above, you'll notice that they are not things that can be definitively proven or disproven. There aren't any tests to confirm whether or not you love someone, or whether or not you're a racist, or whether or not you're going to hell. And, in those cases where there are tests (biopsies and MRIs for cancer, for example), you can't exactly go about performing these tests every second of the day. The minute you're done with that full body MRI scan, might be the moment when you first start developing cancer cells. In other words, if your goal is to stop your intrusive thoughts by disproving them

129

beyond the shadow of a doubt, you will be engaged in this battle with your thoughts for the rest of your life. So, what's the alternative?

The answer is to stop arguing. Accept that these intrusive thoughts are "right" to a certain extent, that all of these things are "possible," and that there is always risk and uncertainty in life. Try taking the following steps in this direction:

1. First off, in the case of medical and safety concerns, take the recommended, reasonable steps to protect yourself and your family. Identify the reasonable precautions for preventing lead exposure. Learn about the physician-recommended measures for preventing cancer. If you are really struggling with intrusive thoughts, these precautions will not, of course, be enough to quiet the intrusive thoughts. Your OCD will still want you to have your house tested for lead paint a second, third, and fourth time, or to google the term "moles and skin cancer" again. But you will now be able to say that you've taken the recommended, reasonable measures and that any additional risks fall under the category of inherent risks of living life.

2. Label the thoughts for what they are. These are not "your" thoughts. These are intrusive thoughts generated by your brain.

   Instead of saying, "I'm worried I don't love my husband."

   Try saying to yourself, "I was having a fine day until I got a little annoyed at my husband for talking during a movie and had the thought in my head that I might not love him."

3. Don't try and disprove the intrusive thought. Acknowledge that the thought could be right. And resist the urge to try argue.

   "You're right, OCD. It's always possible I don't perfectly and fully love my husband right now. But I'm not going to sit here trying to prove it to myself, or to you."

   "Okay brain. There is always a possibility that a mark on my skin could be, or will become, cancerous. But I'm not going to spend the rest of my life worrying about every mark on my skin."

130

"I guess you got me there brain. It's always possible that I could one day "go crazy," but I'm not going to waste the present thinking about it. I'll worry about it when the time comes."

"I can't argue with that. That dust on the counter could have lead dust in it, but it might not. The fact is that dust is everywhere, and I can't go around having all the dust I see tested for lead."

Can you feel the argument in your head being defused already? The fact of the matter is that your intrusive thoughts are a waste of your time. You're probably in love with your husband. You're most likely not going to hell. And you're almost certainly not going to kill someone in the future. But also remember that these things can't ever be proven. Learn to be comfortable with "probably" and "most likely" and you'll be on your way to ending the argument in your head.

Strategy — Maybe / Maybe Not

This one is a slight variation on the Agree with the Possibility" strategy. Whenever you notice yourself trying to disprove a thought, or remove a doubt, you can choose to fully embrace the uncertainty of the thought with the simple statement "Maybe. Maybe not."

"Maybe this person is disrespecting me. Maybe they're not."

"Maybe I'll be successful in OCD treatment. Maybe I won't."

"Maybe I'll get rid of all my OCD. Maybe I'll always have some OCD in my life."

"Maybe tomorrow will be a good day. Maybe it won't."

"Maybe my thoughts can cause things to happen. Maybe they can't."

131

As you can see, the applications of this strategy are endless. Sometimes accepting the uncertainty of a thought, or at least reminding yourself of the futility of disproving a doubt, is just the thing you need to get yourself unstuck.

Strategy — Acceptance

You may at times catch yourself hoping that you'll overcome intrusive thoughts by somehow proving the thoughts wrong or irrational. You'll find yourself looking for that one trick or strategy that will silence the thoughts once and for all, so that the task of resisting rituals will suddenly become easy. It's important to recognize that once you commit yourself to eliminating your responses to these thoughts, that the thoughts don't go away. In fact, your brain can really crank up the volume on all of those warnings and worries and doubts and commands. And the stakes surrounding the decision to ritualize can seem higher than ever.

It's important to temper the expectations when you decide to end a ritualized response to your thoughts. You will continue to encounter all of the risks and scary possibilities and anxiety triggers that have been controlling you up to this point.

The key to not returning to the never-ending loop of your rituals is ACCEPTANCE. You have to make that decision to stop your rituals with an awareness that all of the "What if's," Doubts, and Possibilities will continue to fight for your attention. And the only way to succeed will be to accept the existence of these possibilities, to the point that it no longer matters if they are in your awareness or not. Acceptance simply involves "giving up" the fight. When faced with uncertainty, you allow the uncertainty to exist. You no longer try to avoid it, prevent it, neutralize it, figure it out, fix it, or undo it. And when you encounter risk, you no longer try to eliminate it or wait for it to pass before acting. You accept feeling in danger. You accept feeling uncertain. You accept the feelings and sensations in your body you don't like. And you accept the fact that the bad thing could happen and no amount of ritualizing on your part will ever remove that possibility anyway.

Ultimately, when you start to ACCEPT uncertainty, risk, and unwanted thoughts and feelings, things can change fairly rapidly. You are actually welcoming the reality that your rituals have been helping you artificially avoid. Here are some of those unpleasant realities you may have to work on allowing into your awareness:

- Not knowing for certain what someone else is thinking about you
- Not knowing what the perfect decision will be
- Having someone be upset with you / getting in trouble
- Being judged / someone having a negative thought about you
- Not knowing what germs are in your environment and on your body
- Things not being perfectly fair
- Not liking something about your appearance
- Feeling an uncomfortable, unwanted feeling
- Experiencing an unpleasant and/or embarrassing memory
- Experiencing a change in your routine
- Not having control over something
- Not knowing if, and when, something bad will happen
- Making a mistake / messing up
- Not being perfect
- Not being good at something right away
- Not knowing when you might get sick and/or throw up
- Being uncertain

- Taking a risk

- Not being able to control what thoughts pop into your head

- Not being able to control your feelings

- Having to experience pain and discomfort

- Having OCD

- Having Anxiety

When you successfully start moving towards what's important, it's not because you found out some secret way to remove life's risk and uncertainty. It's because you've decided that there are more important things in life than staying completely safe and avoiding all risk and discomfort.

Step 4   Refocus on Your Goal

Now that you've acknowledged the existence of the thoughts and feelings without trying to eliminate them, you have officially ended your attempts to control those thoughts and feelings. You are allowing them to exist. The next stop is to make sure that those thoughts and feelings don't steer you away from what you were originally doing. In order to stay the course, you will have to allow your unwanted thoughts and feelings to exist for as long as your brain and body want them to continue. Waiting for them to pass simply won't work. And trying to eliminate or reduce them is going to get you stuck ritualizing. So, for this step, don't argue with the thoughts. Don't try and disprove the thoughts. Don't try and reduce the uncomfortable feelings and sensations. Simply make the choice to return your attention back to the thing you were originally doing, even if the thoughts and feelings persist. You are basically allowing that OCD passenger in your life to yell and scream and make a fuss, and then going where you want to go anyway. To really emphasize this step, go ahead and remind yourself what it is you want to do and why you want to do it.

"I'm going to wear my favorite shirt anyway, because I love how soft it is, and it fits me better than any other shirt I own.

"I'm going to the job interview anyway, because having a job and getting a paycheck will feel so good."

"I'm going to drive through the tunnels to get to my brother's house anyway, because it's my niece's birthday and I don't want to miss these precious family moments."

Strategy — Relax Your Brain Muscle

Make a fist and squeeze it as tightly as you can. Notice what it feels like to tighten the muscle of your fingers. Notice the tension. The discomfort. Imagine what would happen if you kept your fist held tightly for an extended period of time. That pain and discomfort would increase. And it would soon be accompanied by intense fatigue in the muscles of your fingers and hand. Now imagine yourself continuing to hold that fist as tightly as you possibly can despite all of that pain and discomfort. If you were to complain to someone about how badly your hand hurt, they'd have a simple answer for you. Why don't you stop making that fist! And if you were to follow that advice, you would feel relief. The pain and exhaustion would quickly subside.

In that way, your brain isn't all that different from the other parts of your body that you control. The difference is that, instead of using muscles, you keep your brain held tight with excessive thinking. All of the following behaviors amount to using your brain muscle:

- Reviewing an idea in your head over and over again

135

- Trying to solve a problem that can't be "solved"
- Trying to figure something out (Am I a bad person? Am I a violent person?
- Searching your memory over and over again
- Trying to predict the future
- Trying to eliminate doubt and uncertainty
- Staying alert and ready for danger
- Trying to control your attention or keep yourself distracted
- Trying to control what thoughts enter your mind

Doing these behaviors repetitively and excessively is the mental equivalent to holding your hand tightly in a fist for hours on end. You are overusing and exhausting your brain. What's more, when you try to achieve something mentally that can't be achieved, you create anxiety. think and think and think, you can actually increase your anxiety. And you also worsen any uncomfortable emotions that the ideas you are reviewing trigger.

Notice when you're flexing that muscle. What does it "feel" like when you are overthinking? Can you "feel" the gears of your mind turning? Is there a tension in your head? Do the muscles in your body tighten up? Does your breathing change? Get to know the sensations so you can catch yourself in problem solving mode.

Realize you have control over your thinking. Earlier in this book, an important distinction was made between thoughts and thinking. Random intrusive thoughts (all of those 'what if's' and doubts that your brain makes you experience) are not in your control. That's your brain trying to alert you to possible danger. Your thinking, on the other hand, is entirely in your control. If you are reviewing, analyzing, or processing the 'what if' thought, you are actively engaging in a behavior that you can stop doing.

Relax your thinking. You now have to simply stop making all of the mental effort. Look at the list of behaviors above and stop each and every one of them. You will have to be thorough in rooting out all of the different effortful mental behaviors. Allow the initial 'what if' intrusive thought to enter and exit your awareness as it wants. Don't focus attention on the thought, but

136

don't focus attention away from it either. Don't do anything at all in response to the intrusive thought. And while the goal is to eventually completely stop all thinking just by simply stopping, you may initially need to prompt yourself. Saying something like "I'm not going to solve that problem," "I'm not going to figure this out," or "I'm not going to keep my guard up" can help you to realize what behaviors you need to stop doing.

Now do whatever you want. You might be asking 'If I can't engage in any of those thinking behaviors, what CAN I do?' And the answer is that you can now do whatever you want with your time, as long as it is not in response to your unwanted intrusive thoughts. Take steps to solve the problem of what drapes you want for the living room, if this is something you can do without repetitively "overthinking." Watch a football game, if this is something you want to do, not something you are using as a distraction from your intrusive thoughts. Focus on relaxing, getting things done, "not caring" about your intrusive thoughts, and living your life.

Strategy — Choose the Here and Now Over Your Imagination

When you experience an intrusive doubt about your experience you are faced with a choice. You can accept the invitation to explore the doubt and follow it into your imagination. Or you can identify the doubt as a misdirection (an Exit Sign) and make the choice to stay in the world of your senses. It's important to recognize that there is NO 3rd option where you follow the doubt into your head, and successfully dismiss it through thinking and logic. Following the doubt will ALWAYS convince you of the worst, not because the worst is actually happening, but because you will encounter an OCD story in your head fueled by anxiety, fear, and other emotions and sensations that will feel real, important, and urgent.

137

Staying in the "here and now" and out of your imagination will require you to make the difficult decision to not engage with the doubt.

When triggered, notice the pull of the urge to ritualize. It will feel like you "should" be doing something. Maybe you should "fix" the situation, maybe you should ruminate or figure something out, maybe you should protect yourself in some way. Before going through with your response, simply notice that urge.

- Notice how you've arrived at a crossroads, with your imagination down one path, and the world of your senses down the other.

- Notice the familiar pull into your imagination. It feels like you might find information there that will help you to figure things out. OCD wants you to believe that intrusive doubts and what if's must be explored. And yet, the only thing that really exists down this path are stories. Nothing more. Nothing less. "What if" leads to "what if" leads to "what if." And none of these "what if's" can ever be disproven. Down the path of your imagination, the story you fear will become the decided and established story.

- Now notice the path of your senses. On the surface it feels like it might not hold enough information. All it promises are your own real-world experiences, and the information you can glean from your senses. In the past you've questioned if that's enough. You've felt that it was important to doubt your senses, and doubt your experience. And yet the path of your senses actually holds MORE information than the world of your imagination, if you'll just let yourself accept it.

- Take a few steps down that path of your senses. Focus your attention on reality. And collect information with your eyes and ears. What is happening right now in the world outside of your head? Identify this information without "thinking" about it or reading into it. Don't try to figure anything out. Don't follow that urge to doubt and make things more complicated. Don't spin a story. And don't doubt the simple, basic facts of the moment. This will only take you into your imagination.

- Now realize that you can stay on this path of your senses if you would like. Doubting the world of the here and now is unhelpful, unnecessary, and, a "wrong turn." There is no need to explore anything other than what is here and now. All you have to do is let yourself stay on this path.

Strategy — Give Yourself Permission to Stop Trying

All of your best intentions, all of your desire to change, all of the words in this book; it's all for naught if deep down you won't ALLOW yourself to stop your ritualizing. Sometimes, you have a motivation for your ritualizing that is at the core of your being and, if unaddressed, will keep you ritualizing no matter how much havoc the behaviors wreak on your life.

- With **moral concerns**, you may fear that you are a bad or sinful person, and this may make you feel like you HAVE to do the rituals to prove you are a good person. Conversely, it may feel like it would confirm you are a bad person if you stopped the ritualizing.

- With **perfectionistic concerns**, you may be struggling with a fear that you lack value as a person. And that any mistakes, or other signs of "failure," are further evidence of this fact. Those perfectionistic thoughts in your head may have even convinced you that "trying" to be perfect is the only thing you have going for you. In other words, if you are intrinsically broken or flawed, at least you're doing something about it. Stopping your rituals may feel like you don't care or are somehow okay with just being a deeply flawed person.

- With **safety concerns**, you fear that you are a danger to yourself or others. Stopping your rituals may feel malicious, uncaring, and

139

irresponsible because, according to the OCD story, you would be removing precautions that are keeping people safe.

If you look at the situations described above, you will notice how the concept of "trying" has become an important strategy for dealing with the fears, and alleviating guilt and anxiety. Trying can really involve anything, but it inevitably means you are "doing something" in response the thoughts and feelings. And so, in order to completely remove your responses to your intrusive thoughts and feelings, you have to completely abandon this idea that "trying" is something important you need to be doing.

Keep that story in check by looking at the world around you. This idea that you have to keep "trying" is based on the premise that the OCD story that you are dangerous, bad, and/or broken is true. If you were to focus solely on the world of your senses, you would notice that you aren't currently convulsing from a pill overdose, aren't currently stabbing someone, aren't currently a complete failure as a human being, aren't currently abusing a child, aren't currently raping someone, etc. etc. etc. (the list could go on). The OCD story is just that; a story unfolding in your head that you are scared might be true, but that you can choose to ignore.

Remember that you are nothing special (in a good way). You are not alone. You are not bearing some heavy individual burden as a bad, dangerous, or flawed human being. We all do "bad" things and feel guilty about them. We all make mistakes. We all have a capacity to do something harmful or dangerous. And we all experience thoughts and feelings that we can't really explain.

You don't have to feel bad. Your OCD obsession may have you convinced that you "should" feel bad about yourself. You may feel an obligation to feel guilty and ashamed because this is what a good and responsible person in your situation should be feeling. But this self-punishment is the behavior of someone who IS guilty, bad, and or worthless. And let's face it. If you're reading this book, there is a part of you that doesn't believe that. Why not try something different. Choose to live as a person who is simply experiencing intrusive doubts about your goodness, competency, or safety. Not as someone who IS these things. Give yourself permission to stop punishing yourself.

Practice Self Compassion. Let go of the guilt and forgive yourself. Be compassionate towards yourself, for having bad thoughts, for making mistakes, for overthinking, for having spent so much time ritualizing and avoidance, for not perfectly implementing the strategy you're reading right now. Allow yourself to gradually get better at not criticizing yourself, and analyzing every move you make. Don't forget that you are a person deserving of the same compassion and understanding as anyone else. You don't have to spend your days endlessly "trying" to do things to punish yourself. Because all you've ever been guilty of is being human.

Live the life you're meant to be living You are not meant to spend your life in your head trying to be certain about things. You are meant to be out there in the world living. Are you ready to finally do the experiment, and find out once and for all if any of the ritualizing and avoidance has been necessary? Everyone is waiting. Your friends. Your family. Your colleagues. Your religious leaders. Everyone's waiting for you to stop living your life based on a story that has unfolded in your head. Once you give up proving something through "trying," you can just be. And that's all anyone has ever wanted from you. So go out there and behave as a person who isn't meant to feel guilty and who doesn't have to endlessly punish themselves. Act like someone who doesn't have to "try." It will feel odd, irresponsible, and reckless at first. But keep it up, and your brain will calm down.

Strategy — Get in Touch With Your Senses

When your OCD thoughts and feelings take hold, the end result is that you can become stuck in your head. This is not an ideal situation because your head is basically OCD's home turf, and if you try to beat OCD with your thoughts vs. his thoughts, you will find yourself at a serious disadvantage. In this situation, it is often critical that you take a moment and focus on the one thing that can pull you back into the world around you: your senses. There are plenty of strategies to do this, and often it's as simple as having a number of coping skills at your disposal that are sensory in nature. Having paints, clay, a pad and paper, or a musical instrument ready to go can really help you reconnect with the world around you and get unstuck from your head. Additionally, here's another simple exercise that you can complete literally anywhere without needing any supplies. This is simply about "noticing" what your senses are picking up. As you complete the exercise, notice how it completely engages and distracts your mind and connects you with the world outside of your head:

1. Find 5 things you can see

2. Find 4 things you can touch

3. Find 3 things you can hear

4. Find 2 things you can smell

5. Find 1 thing you can taste

Make sure you don't simply identify the sensory items but that you actually follow through and use your senses (pick up the pencil you found and smell it, touch the fabric of the chair you're sitting on, etc.). Focus all of your attention on your senses. Notice the varied sensory experiences and appreciate them. Once you reconnect with your surroundings, you're ready to follow through with Step 4 and Refocus on Your Goal. With a little practice, you'll be resisting that urge to engage with OCD thoughts and increasing the amount of time you spend on your own goals.

Step 5 — TOLERATE DISCOMFORT

Here we are at the final step of the START method, and it's not exactly an easy one. In fact, for many, this step can be the most difficult. Challenging OCD requires you to resist your rituals and stop yourself from mentally engaging with your thoughts and feelings for extended periods of time. When you first start challenging an OCD obsession, this can lead to significant distress. When OCD senses your attempts to go your own way, he can really dial up the thoughts, feelings, urges, and sensations, in an effort to regain your commitment to his agenda. And yet, to really complete the START method and take your life back from OCD, you have to find the will and the courage to push through all of that discomfort.

You might say that step 5 is simple, but not easy. It's simple because it just involves tolerating the uncomfortable experience of being triggered and, instead of doing anything to make it stop, waiting for the discomfort to pass with time. It's difficult because you have to experience some pretty uncomfortable feelings and sensations. The good news is that this treatment approach works. The more you practice experiencing that discomfort, the easier it becomes, and the less power OCD has over you. And you will discover that this is all OCD has ever had at his disposal. He's been able to put some thoughts in your head, and he's been able to make you feel some uncomfortable emotions. And that's it. Show OCD that you can handle those thoughts and feelings, and OCD no longer has anything against you. With that in mind, here are a few more strategies that you can use to help you find success in Tolerating Discomfort.

Strategy — Think of Your Emotions as Weather Patterns

One of the most important realizations you may have while learning to manage your OCD is that your feelings and emotions are not in your control. Your brain and your body decide what emotion you will be feeling at any given moment in time. And they don't check in with you before making their decision. One of the most helpful metaphors available for developing a healthy and realistic relationship with your emotions is that your emotions are like the weather – no more controllable, no more predictable, and (on a positive note) no more permanent. Your emotions pass with time, without requiring any action on your part. Emotions are temporary signals. And if we allow ourselves to experience them, rather than try to control them through rituals and avoidance, they pass all on their own. To help remind yourself of this fact, it can be useful to think of your emotions as weather patterns.

- Your sadness is a Sunday morning shower.

- Your anxiety is a thunderstorm.

- Your anger is like the waves crashing violently against the rocks during a coastal storm.

- Your lack of motivation is an early morning fog.

- Your embarrassment is a dark overcast sky.

- And soon it will end. The sun will return. The waves will calm. The fog will lift.

The key is to let the emotions happen. Notice where in your body they show up and what they feel like. And then accept the physical sensations. Be sure not to put any restrictions on your emotions. Many a person has made their anxiety worse by thinking things such as "I have to make sure this anxiety goes away before my test" or "I have to be feeling completely calm

144

when I talk to my boss today.". This is trying to exert emotional control, and it's the opposite of how you generally think of the weather. You would never mentally or physically try to stop it from snowing or raining. You wouldn't attempt to convince the temperature to change. And your naturally occurring and somewhat unpredictable emotions are no different. So let it rain, sleet, or storm when it needs to. Make peace with the turbulent world of your emotions.

Strategy Don't Completely Trust Your Feelings (At Least When it Comes to Your Obsessions)

When faced with the choice between doing a ritual like completing a 10-minute ritualized hand wash or feeling the guilt and anxiety that will result from resisting this urge, it makes sense that you would get in the habit of performing the ritual. But once you commit to challenging OCD, you realize that the only way to take back control of your life is to begin the work of resisting your rituals. One of the biggest challenges is figuring out how to do so in the face of those extreme emotions OCD is throwing at you. Let's look at some steps you can take to not fall for the trap of believing all of those emotions and allowing them to control you.

Realize that Star Wars was wrong: In modern culture, we receive a lot of encouragement for listening to our emotions. Who hasn't been told to follow their passion, or listen to their heart? In the iconic Star Wars movies, the characters are fond of telling each other to search their feelings. And, let's face it, sometimes it feels really good to completely give in to our emotions and let them guide us. Unfortunately, when you have OCD there is a little glitch in your brain that is causing you to have certain feelings at the wrong time. You're feeling guilty when you've done nothing wrong. You're feeling disgusted when you're not actually dirty. You're feeling anxious and panicked when no one is in danger. One of the keys to successfully battling OCD is to

145

learn NOT to trust the emotional signals your brain is sending you, at least when it comes to your specific OCD obsessions. This requires you to create some distance between yourself and your feelings. The next time your OCD is triggered, be sure NOT to search your feelings. DON'T ask yourself questions like: "Why do I feel so anxious?" "What did I do wrong this time?" This will only lead to getting stuck in your head with your OCD thoughts. Instead, remind yourself that "This is just my OCD making me feel this uncomfortable physical sensation at the wrong time.

Get good at feeling bad: Once you start to question the signals your brain is sending you, the battle is far from over. Your OCD is going to keep making you feel the uncomfortable feeling for a while. This means that, while you have to stop searching your feelings and figuring out what they might mean, you still have to accept their existence. This will involve increasing your tolerance for the uncomfortable feelings you've been trying to get rid of all these years. Some of the bad feelings that OCD sufferers have to feel include anger, guilt, anxiety, sadness, and disgust. Whatever emotions your OCD has been torturing you with, try to get in touch with the physical experience of these emotions. Instead of fighting the physical experiences, make room for them. Notice where in your body they happen. Loosen up your muscles and let the sensations spread and disperse. The physical experience is often more tolerable than you realize, especially when you stop analyzing your feelings and trying to figure out what they mean. If you were busy with something before you were triggered (doing homework, talking to someone, etc.) try and redirect your attention back to the activity, even if the uncomfortable feelings remain. And if you're not busy with anything, see if there is something you can occupy yourself with. Just try and resist your typical OCD rituals. And don't wait for the feelings to pass. Accept them. And get back to living life.

Strategy Get Ready for a 2nd, 3rd, and Maybe Even a 4th Wave of Thoughts

When you set limits with your OCD, one thing that OCD likes to do in retaliation is expand on the intrusive thoughts and increase the stakes. OCD basically says "Okay, so you think you can challenge that thought? Well, how about this one?" Tolerating this second round of thoughts (and the 3rd, 4th, 5th, etc.) can be the really difficult part of challenging OCD. Basically, while you may be fully ready to challenge the initial thought you're challenging, these subsequent thoughts catch you off guard. Here are some examples of thoughts that OCD likes to throw around when it senses a challenge:

- You're being extremely neglectful and irresponsible to not be listening to me.

- That was a bad decision not to do your rituals. You are currently doing damage to yourself and others.

- You've already screwed things up, but it's not too late. You can fix it.

- If you stop what you're doing now, you may even be able to reverse things, if you work especially hard at ritualizing.

- The longer you put this off, the more permanent damage will happen.

- Sure, in the past some of your rituals turned out to be unnecessary. But this time it's different. This time it's real, and you are going to regret not doing anything about this.

- You do realize you don't have OCD, don't you? You are choosing to ignore an actual, real threat.

- Agreeing to do this exposure is just another example of you messing things up like you always do. You make bad decisions. You always end up being wrong. You can't trust yourself. You're better off completing your rituals. Then at least you can say you've done all you can.

147

- Just face it. You can't handle this exposure stuff. You can't handle anxiety. It's not worth it.

- This anxiety is never going to stop. This habituation thing will never happen for you.

- You will regret this for the rest of your life.

- This time it's real. You have to do it.

- Don't take the chance. You'll never forgive yourself.

- You can't be anxious today. There are too many important things happening. You have to do your rituals.

I think you get the point. And you're probably more than familiar with this line of thinking from your OCD. So, what's the key to dealing with these multiple rounds of thoughts? You use the principles of the START method that you would use with any other OCD thoughts. You go right back to Accepting your thoughts and feelings, Refocusing on your goal, and Tolerating the discomfort.

You're not going to always be perfect at this. You're going to have missteps. OCD is going to win sometimes. And that's okay. The important thing is that you maintain your awareness each day. You notice when you're responding to your thoughts. You notice when you're ritualizing. And you take the time to see how much time this is taking away from the other things you want to be doing. And, each day, you commit to getting a little bit better at utilizing these strategies and taking your life back from OCD.

Exercise: Develop Your START Strategy

To complete this chapter, you'll find a START worksheet below that you can use to formulate your START plan in response to various aspects of your OCD. You'll also find some examples of some completed START worksheets to demonstrate how to effectively complete them with various OCD presentations.

START

TO TAKE LIFE BACK FROM OCD

1. SET YOUR DESTINATION

I WANT TO LEARN HIP-HOP DANCING.

IDENTIFY YOUR GOAL HERE

2. TAKE STEPS TOWARDS YOUR GOAL

I'M GOING TO TAKE SOME FREE VIRTUAL LESSONS ONLINE

LIST CONCRETE ACTIONS YOU CAN TAKE TOWARDS YOUR GOAL

3. ACKNOWLEDGE OCD THOUGHTS AND FEELINGS

I'M HAVING THOUGHTS THAT I'M NOT LEARNING THE MOVES QUICKLY ENOUGH,

THAT THIS IS JUST ANOTHER THING I'M AWFUL AT, THAT I'M WORSE AT THINGS

THAN OTHER PEOPLE, AND THAT I'LL NEVER "MASTER" ANYTHING

LIST THE THOUGHTS AND FEELINGS YOU CAN EXPECT TO HAVE WHEN TAKING ACTION

4. REFOCUS ON YOUR GOAL

I DON'T NEED TO "MASTER" HIP-HOP DANCING. I JUST WANT TO LEARN THE

BASICS. I'M GOING TO FOCUS ON LEARNING ONE MOVE TODAY.

WRITE A REMINDER STATEMENT OF YOUR GOAL, AND WHY YOU WANT TO CHOOSE YOUR
GOAL OVER OCD

5. TOLERATE DISCOMFORT

I FEEL BAD ABOUT MYSELF BECAUSE I'M NOT TRYING TO "MASTER" THE DANCE.

WHAT UNWANTED FEELINGS WILL YOU HAVE TO ACCEPT AS YOU FOCUS ON YOUR GOAL?

START

TO TAKE LIFE BACK FROM OCD

1. SET YOUR DESTINATION

I WANT TO WRITE MY PAPER FOR HISTORY.

IDENTIFY YOUR GOAL HERE

2. TAKE STEPS TOWARDS YOUR GOAL

I'M GOING TO SIT DOWN AND START WRITING AN INTRODUCTION.

LIST CONCRETE ACTIONS YOU CAN TAKE TOWARDS YOUR GOAL

3. ACKNOWLEDGE OCD THOUGHTS AND FEELINGS

OCD IS MAKING ME THINK ABOUT ALL OF THE SOURCES I WILL NEED TO FIND,

HOW I NEED TO COME UP WITH A BRILLIANT IDEA, HOW I MIGHT NOT GET INTO

COLLEGE, AND END UP JOBLESS ON THE STREET, AND A COMPLETE FAILURE.

LIST THE THOUGHTS AND FEELINGS YOU CAN EXPECT TO HAVE WHEN TAKING ACTION

4. REFOCUS ON YOUR GOAL

I WANT TO SIMPLY FOCUS ON MY INTRODUCTION. I WANT TO BE MORE PRODUCTIVE

IN LIFE. ENGAGING WITH ALL OF MY OCD THOUGHTS USUALLY JUST LEADS TO ME

PROCRASTINATING AND GETTING NOTHING DONE. I'LL FOCUS ON THE FIRST STEP.

WRITE A REMINDER STATEMENT OF YOUR GOAL, AND WHY YOU WANT TO CHOOSE YOUR
GOAL OVER OCD

5. TOLERATE DISCOMFORT

I HAVE TO FEEL ANXIOUS AND IMPATIENT TO BE SO FAR FROM FINISHING MY PAPER.

WHAT UNWANTED FEELINGS WILL YOU HAVE TO ACCEPT AS YOU FOCUS ON YOUR GOAL?

START

TO TAKE LIFE BACK FROM OCD

1. **SET YOUR DESTINATION**

   I WANT TO EXPAND MY DIET TO MORE THAN JUST ENSURE AND CEREAL.

   IDENTIFY YOUR GOAL HERE

2. **TAKE STEPS TOWARDS YOUR GOAL**

   I'M GOING TO EAT A FEW BITES OF TUNA FISH TODAY.

   LIST CONCRETE ACTIONS YOU CAN TAKE TOWARDS YOUR GOAL

3. **ACKNOWLEDGE OCD THOUGHTS AND FEELINGS**

   OCD IS TELLING ME THAT THE CAN OF TUNA COULD HAVE BEEN IMPROPERLY

   SEALED. IF THAT'S THE CASE, IT COULD BE CONTAMINATED WITH DANGEROUS

   BACTERIA. IT COULD KILL ME. I SHOULDN'T TAKE THE CHANCE.

   LIST THE THOUGHTS AND FEELINGS YOU CAN EXPECT TO HAVE WHEN TAKING ACTION

4. **REFOCUS ON YOUR GOAL**

   I'M GOING TO OPEN A CAN OF TUNA FISH AND EAT IT. I'M NOT GOING TO ENGAGE

   WITH ALL OF OCD'S WORRIES. I LOVE TUNA FISH AND I HAVE TO TAKE THIS STEP

   TO BE ABLE TO EAT THE FOODS I ENJOY AGAIN.

   WRITE A REMINDER STATEMENT OF YOUR GOAL, AND WHY YOU WANT TO CHOOSE YOUR
   GOAL OVER OCD

5. **TOLERATE DISCOMFORT**

   I HAVE TO FEEL SCARED AND FEEL LIKE I ABSOLUTELY SHOULD NOT EAT THIS.

   WHAT UNWANTED FEELINGS WILL YOU HAVE TO ACCEPT AS YOU FOCUS ON YOUR GOAL?

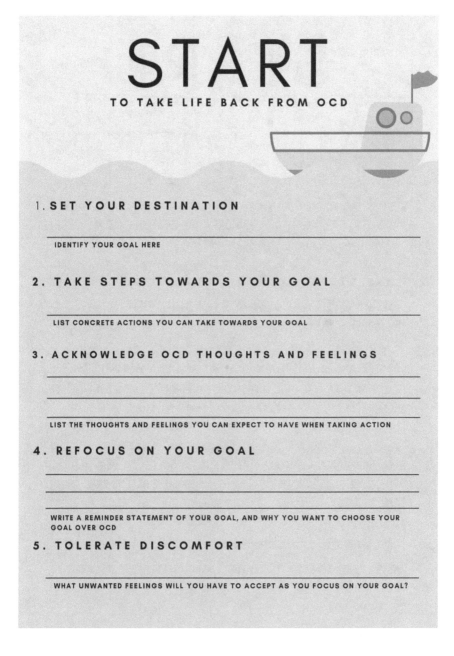

START

TO TAKE LIFE BACK FROM OCD

1. SET YOUR DESTINATION

IDENTIFY YOUR GOAL HERE

2. TAKE STEPS TOWARDS YOUR GOAL

LIST CONCRETE ACTIONS YOU CAN TAKE TOWARDS YOUR GOAL

3. ACKNOWLEDGE OCD THOUGHTS AND FEELINGS

LIST THE THOUGHTS AND FEELINGS YOU CAN EXPECT TO HAVE WHEN TAKING ACTION

4. REFOCUS ON YOUR GOAL

WRITE A REMINDER STATEMENT OF YOUR GOAL, AND WHY YOU WANT TO CHOOSE YOUR GOAL OVER OCD

5. TOLERATE DISCOMFORT

WHAT UNWANTED FEELINGS WILL YOU HAVE TO ACCEPT AS YOU FOCUS ON YOUR GOAL?

Available for download at *https://pittsburghocdtreatment.com/publications/the-ocd-travel-guide/*

Chapter 5

Exposure and Response Prevention (Pointing Your Compass Directly at What Makes You Anxious)

Exposure and Response Prevention (ERP) is the number one recommended treatment for OCD. Whenever you are seeking out mental health treatment for your OCD, always make sure that it is with a provider who is well versed in this treatment. ERP is based on the strategy of using "exposures" to increase your tolerance for triggers and gradually reduce the anxiety and distress you are experiencing in life. It is extremely effective and, in fact, thanks to developments in ERP over the past 30 years or so, OCD is now considered an extremely treatable mental health issue. While the reality for most people with OCD is that they will never really be "cured" of OCD, a vast majority who engage in ERP will experience a dramatic reduction in their OCD symptoms. In many cases, it is possible to eliminate obsessions to the point that they no longer bother you on a regular basis. And in most other cases, you can reduce them to the point that, while they might still bother you a bit, you still feel like you have regained control over those parts of your life that were being impacted.

If you have already been practicing the START method, then congratulations, you have already been doing exposures. Any time you are triggered and, instead of ritualizing and avoiding, stay in the triggering situation and wait for your thoughts and feelings to subside all on their own, you are engaging in exposure therapy. The name ERP says it all. You undergo Exposure (E) to your triggers and then commit yourself to Response Prevention (RP), which is another way of saying you resist your rituals. So far, we have focused most of our discussion on how to approach "natural exposures," which are exposures that naturally occur during the day whenever you happen upon a trigger. Now we are going to focus some attention on the process of setting up "planned exposures."

When it comes to overcoming OCD, and anxiety in general, exposure IS ultimately the answer. The more frequently and consistently you engage in exposures, the more rapidly you can expect to see a reduction in your symptoms, and the more significant this reduction will be. With this principle in mind, it is usually not enough to wait around to be triggered before you practice resisting your rituals. You will need to expedite the OCD treatment process by engaging in planned exposures that you design and put into place. Planned exposures target your OCD fears in a very systematic and deliberate way. Examples of planned exposures include 1) purposefully holding your hand on a toilet flush handle for 10 minutes if you are struggling with contamination concerns in the bathroom or 2) saying your prayer the "wrong" way if you are experiencing religious fears of God rejecting you in some way. These planned experiences give you the opportunity to face your fears in a more controlled and intensive way. You get to decide on when you complete the exposures, how difficult they are, and how long they last. These exposures are repeated over and over again, and then gradually intensified at a pace with which you are comfortable. There are 2 reasons to include planned exposures in your OCD management plan:

1. **Just "living life" doesn't provide you with enough exposure:** When you have an OCD obsession, you are basically stuck with an extreme and exaggerated fear. And just going about your life normally might not provide you with the frequency and breadth of exposures required to effectively treat your fear. In other words, if you want to overcome a fear of heights, you're going to have to purposefully go up to those high places as much as you possibly can.

2. **The "exposures" that life is throwing at you are too difficult a starting point.** When OCD disrupts your life, you can become so overwhelmed by your symptoms that you are forced to retreat from certain areas of life. When this happens, simply going back to living normally is not going to happen overnight. You will need to specifically design baby-step exposures that will allow you to work your way up to the more difficult exposure you will face in the real world. For example, if you are experiencing obsessions around food contamination, you

may have to set up some controlled exposures to different types of food at home before you eat at a restaurant.

Up until this point, OCD has had one overarching goal for you: Avoid things that make you uncomfortable, uncertain, anxious, and at risk. He's had you pointing your compass directly away from these things. The problem, of course, is that discomfort, uncertainty, anxiety, and risk are essential elements of life. They are a part of everyday experience. And so, OCD has effectively had you pointing your compass away from life. Here are some of the things that OCD has had you pointing yourself away from:

- Away from Fear
- Away from Anxiety
- Away from Physical Discomfort
- Away from Worry
- Away from Unwanted Thoughts
- Away from Unwanted Emotions
- Away from Risk
- Away from Doubt
- Away from Uncertainty

And where exactly has OCD been pointing you towards? The answer is simple. Nowhere in particular. OCD hasn't been concerned with where you end up, as long as it's as far away from your triggers as possible. If that leads you to living in one corner of your bedroom and never leaving that spot, OCD has absolutely no problem with that. If it leads to you not setting any educational or career goals for yourself, OCD's fine with that. If your relationships fail, if you fail to make new friends, if you don't find a romantic partner, if you don't try out for any sports teams, if you drop out of college, none of that will bother OCD, as long as you keep moving away from the anxiety and discomfort,

155

To deal with this problem, you're going to have to point your compass directly at those things you've been avoiding. Exposure and Response Prevention is all about going out of your way to purposefully do the things that make you anxious, uncomfortable, and uncertain. And what happens next is the truly amazing part of this treatment. You gradually find the bravery to face your fears, you increase your tolerance of discomfort, and you make peace with uncertainty. As you design and complete exposures, you're going to get really good at experiencing things and feeling things that currently feel intolerable. You're going to get good at being uncertain, uncomfortable, at risk, and imperfect. You can think of it as a sort of like an inoculation. You're going to be giving yourself a vaccine against all of the anguish you've been experiencing as a result of your OCD. And you're going to come out on the other end stronger than you ever imagined you could be.

Safety Learning Vs. Danger Learning (Reversing the OCD Trend)

As someone struggling with OCD obsessions, you are essentially stuck with fears that you never asked for. And it's important that you understand how fear works in the brain, if you're going to understand why exposure therapy is necessary. Keep in mind that your goal is essentially to reduce the fear response your brain is having to certain stimuli. You want to stop being anxious every time you see a bible or hear the word pedophile or think of germs. You don't want to have to obsess over these things anymore.

As you probably already know all too well, the brain is extremely quick when it comes to Fear Learning. The brain can develop a new fear from just a single bad incident, and it will spread that fear far and wide. So, if you get food poisoning after eating at a seafood restaurant, you'll obviously never want to go to that specific seafood restaurant ever again. But you may also notice your brain is suddenly wanting you to avoid all seafood restaurants. And your brain may even go to extremes and make you hesitant to go to restaurants in general. That's just the way that fear learning works. And, if you really think about it, it makes total sense from a survival perspective. Your brain has one goal. Keep you safe, and don't take any chances. Your brain doesn't want you to almost die from a snake bite and then go out the next day and pet a snake. Your brain wants you to stay far away from all snakes. And it doesn't want you making any judgment calls on the matter. Now, as someone with OCD, you are struggling with a fear that wasn't necessarily established from an initial bad experience. But you've still undoubtedly experienced your brain's tendency to spread fears quite judiciously to various areas of your life, even if it's an OCD fear you've randomly acquired.

By engaging in exposure therapy, you are activating the brain's opposing mechanism, it's Safety Learning tendency (Yes. It exists!). The important thing to note about Safety Learning is that it occurs much more slowly than Danger Learning. Your brain doesn't like to let go of a fear simply because you've had one positive experience. So, if you go to a seafood restaurant once and don't get sick? Great. But don't expect the anxiety to be any less the next time you go back to that restaurant. In fact, the first, second, third, fourth, and fifth times you visit that seafood restaurant, you may continue to feel fear and anxiety at the same intensity. And yet, your brain WILL eventually change if you stick with it. You just have to push through those initial difficulties and allow your brain to realize that the past is the past, and seafood restaurants are now safe once more. The other important thing to know about safety learning: it does not generalize like your learned fears do. If you go to *Red Lobster* over and over again, your brain may simply decide that *Red Lobster* appears to be safe. But those other seafood restaurants around town? Not so much. You may have to desensitize yourself to a few more restaurants before the fear completely fades.

Did I mention that Exposure Therapy is hard work? Yeah. But it's also hard work that pays off. And when faced with the choice of living with endless obsessing vs. engaging in exposure therapy, the choice is usually simple. And you will overcome those fears if you set your mind to it. So, let's get started!

Developing a Personalized ERP Plan

In this section, you will be learning how to develop your own personalized ERP plan, so that you can guide your own exposure treatment. On paper, ERP is a fairly straightforward idea. You identify all of the things that your OCD is making it hard to do, and you start to do those things in a systematic way, while resisting all of your usual OCD rituals. Here are the typical steps in an ERP protocol:

1. **Complete a Full Assessment of Your OCD Symptoms**

2. **Identify Coping Skills**

3. **Address Any Special Considerations Before Engaging in Exposure Therapy**

4. **Fear Hierarchy Development**

5. **Begin Exposures**

6. **Fine Tune the Exposure Process**

Step 1: Complete a Full Assessment of OCD Symptoms

If you've been working through the exercises in this book, you've already completed a pretty thorough assessment of your OCD symptoms. In particular, identifying your own Cycle of Avoidance in Chapter 2 includes all of your core OCD symptoms: 1) your triggers, 2) your intrusive thoughts, 3) your triggered feelings, and 4) your rituals. If you've completed this step, you have a very good understanding of your OCD. In order to begin the ERP process, you're going to want to take this information and format it in a way that will help you come up with exposures.

Exercise: Complete the ERP Brainstorm Worksheet

On the pages ahead you will find the ERP Brainstorm assessment form. This will help you prepare for Step 4 when you begin identifying exposures. Here are the instructions for completing the worksheet.

Themes: In this box, fill out the general theme of your fears. You can be general (contamination) or a little more specific (food-borne pathogens) if you think it will help you zero in on exposure ideas.

Things I Am Currently Avoiding: Here you will identify all of the people, places, objects, activities, places, media, words, thoughts, physical sensations, and emotions you are currently avoiding. Sometimes it can be difficult to notice your own avoidance because it can become stealthily woven into the everyday life you've established for yourself. Be sure to think about all of the things in life you are currently not doing (i.e., using public restrooms, exercising, eating at restaurants) and then imagine what it would be like to do these things. If you don't think it would be a big deal to do these things, then there is probably a non-OCD explanation for why you're not doing it. However, if it makes you anxious, stressed, and worried to think about doing any of these things, then there is a good chance you are avoiding these things, and you should add them to the list.

My Current Rituals and Triggers: Here you will develop a thorough list of your rituals (physical and mental) and then identify the triggers that usually cause you to engage in these rituals. So, for example, if you have to engage in an extended hand wash after coming home from school, you would indicate "extended hand wash" in the ritual column and "arriving home after school" in the trigger column. The more detailed and specific you can be with your rituals, the easier it will be to come up with exposures. So, instead of "extended hand wash" you may want to write "Scrub each fingernail for 20 seconds, wash the back of each hand for 10 seconds, washing my palms for 10 seconds, rinse, and then repeat this a total of 5 times."

Once you've completed the ERP Brainstorm worksheet, hold onto it for the moment. You'll be referring back to it during Step 4, Fear Hierarchy Development.

ERP BRAINSTORM

My Obsessional Themes	

Things I'm currently trying to avoid (including people, places, objects, activities, thoughts, emotions, and physical sensations	

Ritual	Trigger

Available for download at *https://pittsburghocdtreatment.com/publications/the-ocd-travel-guide/*

160

ERP BRAINSTORM

Ritual	Trigger

Available for download at *https://pittsburghocdtreatment.com/publications/the-ocd-travel-guide/*

Step 2: Identify Coping Skills

Your coping skills are those activities you have at your disposal that allow you to cope and manage difficult emotional experiences without turning to your rituals. This is a critical step because putting yourself through exposures is very difficult work, and you're going to want to have coping activities available without you having to go searching in the moment. Good coping skills tend to be activities that are tactile in nature such as painting, shooting hoops, or playing with your dog. However, for some, more intellectual pursuits such as reading may still be workable. Just be careful with thinking activities since the brain is OCD's turf and it is easy to get lost in OCD thoughts when you are already engaged in a mental activity. Your coping skills are going to help you in 2 ways: 1) They instill some general enjoyment into your day as you begin the daily work of challenging your OCD and 2) they provide you with a coping option in those rare moments when you engage in an exposure and find yourself feeling overwhelmed. Keep in mind that you should never go into an exposure planning to use a coping skill, and you really shouldn't have to turn to them regularly as long as you are choosing exposures you are willing and able to complete. But in those rare moments when you start an exposure and feel overly triggered, a coping skill is the preferred method (over ritualizing) for dealing with the emotional discomfort, since using a coping skill will not reinforce your obsession the way that rituals do.

There is nothing all that complicated about this step, but make sure you do take the time to complete it. Think about your interests, your current environment, and what generally works for you to manage stress, anxiety, anger and other difficult emotions. Make sure you are identifying activities that are NOT rituals. In other words, they should not be activities that directly respond to your OCD fears and somehow serve to neutralize intrusive thoughts. So, going for a walk is a great coping skill. But praying to alleviate OCD worries that I'm going to hell is definitely not a coping skill. In general, consider coping skills in the following areas:

1. Exercise and physical activity: These are great coping skills. Not only are you engaged in activities that get you "out of your head," but you are burning calories, staying healthy, and letting off steam.

2. The arts and creative pursuits: This is another area that is full of great coping skill options. Focusing your mind on a task like "I'm going to finish this portrait" or "I'm going to write a poem" is a great way to set goals that provide your life with meaning and channel your emotions in a positive direction.

3. Domestic pursuits: Cooking, cleaning, home improvement projects. All of these things can get your mind focused on engaging tasks.

4. Entertainment and media: Video games, internet sites and TV/Movies can be great coping skills. Just be careful not to focus on pursuits that end up consuming large parts of your day and detracting from the learning you need your mind to do while you are challenging your OCD. If you complete exposures and then immediately start playing video games for 3 hours, you may be engaging in intense distraction to the point that your brain is not learning from the exposure process as much as it could be. As basic as this advice might sound, just remember, everything in moderation.

If you identify coping skills that you would like to utilize, don't forget to make sure you have the needed supplies. Take the time to go to the art supplies store or the sporting goods store or log onto Amazon and purchase that sketchbook or basketball or bag of seeds for the vegetable garden. You'll be glad you did!

Step 3: Address Any Special Considerations Before Engaging in Exposure Therapy

Depression: If you are currently struggling with a significant bout of depression, don't hesitate to connect with a mental health professional before you jump into ERP therapy. ERP is hard work and takes a toll on your mental resources. It is also not really geared towards helping people overcome depression. You can always come back to ERP once you've reduced your depression symptoms.

Another consideration, however, is that sometimes it is one's OCD symptoms that are causing the depression. If you feel that this describes you, then you may want to give ERP a try and see if challenging OCD is the thing that starts to make you feel less depressed. Again, though, if ERP seems to make matters worse, there is no shame in finding help for your symptoms of depression first.

Eating Behaviors: If you are struggling with maladaptive eating behaviors such that you meet criteria for an Eating Disorder, it may be advisable to engage in focused Eating Disorder treatment first (with clinicians who also have some understanding of OCD). This will ensure that you stabilize your weight and health and can be mentally and physically prepared to complete ERP for your OCD symptoms. Since both issues are debilitating and can greatly overlap, you may also find yourself needing to engage in treatment for both issues simultaneously.

Suicidality and Self-Harm: If you are currently experiencing intent to attempt suicide, or you are engaged in cutting behavior, you should, first and foremost, be under the regular care of a mental health professional and only be engaging in specific mental health interventions based on their guidance. As someone with OCD, it is also important that your therapist and/or psychiatrist have knowledge of OCD and ERP so that they can properly differentiate between genuine suicidal ideology and intrusive OCD fears of being suicidal.

Reasonable Precautions: If you are struggling with an obsession that is an exaggerated fear of a real-life threat, like medical conditions or lead paint contamination, you may be struggling to figure out how much of your worrying is "normal" and how much is "OCD." In these situations, you have to take the important first step to identify the normal, reasonable precautions you should take to avoid the threat. This involves researching the topic online or talking to a professional or authority in the area of concern. Looking to the EPA's recommended precautions to prevent lead paint exposure. Talk to a doctor about what you can do to screen yourself for cancer. And talk to a priest or other religious figure about how often you're supposed to complete your sanctioned religious (non-OCD) rituals like praying or going to confession. This will allow you to draw a line in the sand. On one side are the reasonable steps you SHOULD take. On the other side are the excessive steps that OCD wants you to take. Behaviors in this second group can all be grouped into the OCD ritual category.

Knowing What Emotions to Expect: This has already been mentioned but is worth reiterating here. OCD was until recently categorized as an Anxiety Disorder. It is now its own category because the mental health field acknowledged that not everyone experiences anxiety when triggered. Many people with contamination concerns struggle with Disgust when triggered. Others who have Perfectionism OCD can experience strong negative emotions directed at themselves, similar to depression, when triggered. Still others experience anger, shame, guilt, jealousy, and "not just right" feelings. Make sure that you recognize the emotions your OCD makes you feel. This is going to be important when you start exposures, because a lot of these emotions will make you feel like something is wrong. You may be tempted to think that exposure therapy isn't working because it's not making me anxious, it's just making me angry or making me feel bad about myself. The reality, however, is that if those are your triggered emotions, that is exactly what you are meant to be experiencing during exposures. Going into exposures with this expectation will help you stick with the treatment long enough for the reduction in your symptoms to start to take effect.

An Important Note on Scrupulosity Obsessions: If you are experiencing fears around going to hell, accidentally making a promise to Satan, or doing something that may be sacrilegious, it's important that you come into exposures ready to do what it takes to overcome your fear. This means that it is important that you separate your spiritual intentions (you want to have a relationship with God) from your engagement in exposure therapy for your OCD (you want to overcome your OCD fears). Keep in mind that your OCD has infiltrated your spiritual life to the point that you can't function in this area. You are going to have to engage in scrupulosity exposures to overcome your fears in this area, and by definition this will involve doing things that are

165

"sacrilegious," so that you can live without overwhelming fear in your spiritual life. If you do not take the steps to complete these exposures, your OCD fears will continue to control you in this area of your life. As you consider developing exposures, ask yourself the following questions:

- Would God want you to complete the proper treatment for your OCD symptoms?

- Will s/he understand why you are completing exposures to target your religious fears?

If you still have confusion in this area, be sure to consult with a religious authority on how you can properly engage in exposure therapy and still practice your faith. Many religious leaders receive training in OCD scrupulosity so, if possible, see if you can find someone who has heard of OCD with religious themes. And don't be afraid to consult with a mental health professional versed in OCD and discuss with them your concerns with engaging in religious exposures.

It is also important to recognize that there is often religious pressure to have absolute, unshakeable faith, which is essentially pressure to attain certainty. While this sort of certainty may work fine for someone without OCD, keep in mind that they are not living with the OCD pressure to have absolute, 100% certainty. As individuals not experiencing OCD scrupulosity, they are simply fine with the relative certainty they are able to attain. As a religious person living with OCD, your path with your religion is going to look different. You will have to make peace with the inevitable uncertainty around spiritual matters, even around the big questions like if God even exists and make the choice to practice your beliefs without trying to remove this uncertainty.

Step 4: Fear Hierarchy Development

Developing a thorough Fear Hierarchy (aka Fear Ladder) is an essential first step in ERP that can make the rest of the process that much easier. Your fear ladder is essentially the personalized list of exposures you have identified to specifically target your OCD obsessions. Through a creative brainstorming process, you identify a range of exposures, and then rank them in order of difficulty. A good fear ladder has as many diverse exposures as you can identify, and a good variety of difficulty levels. Someone with contamination concerns, for example, might identify 'Not washing my hands before I brush my teeth' and rank this exposure as a 3 out of 10 difficulty. They might then identify "using a public restroom" as a 9 out of 10. Another important step in developing a fear ladder is to identify all of the rituals that you must refrain from completing during exposures. The person above who is dealing with contamination fears might identify "using my sleeve as a barrier when opening doors" and "holding my breath when near people" as rituals they must commit to resisting while doing their exposures.

Identifying Exposures

Your exposure list should be as expansive and thorough as possible. Difficulty should range from exposures you would feel comfortable doing right now to exposures you don't think you'll ever want to do. Don't let this make you too nervous. This is all part of the process. As you think of harder exposures to add to the list, keep in mind you're never obligated to do an exposure just because you've identified it. But you also don't want to leave anything off the table. Once you get traction with exposure work, you'll become surprised by what you're willing to do in the future. As you start to think about potential exposures to properly target your OCD, here are a few places to jumpstart the brainstorming process:

What Is Currently Difficult To Do? This is the question at the core of all exposure therapy. Coming up with answers to this question can immediately lead to potential exposures. Things like using dishes in my home, wearing a certain t-shirt, attending a religious service, and eating a certain food item are all exposures that can result from asking yourself this question.

Do the Opposite: Another simple principle to live by when it comes to exposure development is to simply do the opposite of what your OCD wants

167

you to do. OCD wants you to avoid that television program? Watch it. OCD doesn't want you to think about that possibility? Force yourself to think about it on purpose. OCD insists you find someone or something to give you reassurance for your worries? Don't reassure yourself at all. This is pretty much the core principle of exposure identification.

Changing, Delaying, or Limiting Rituals: It's important to recognize that you can't always just completely eliminate your rituals. This is often a big step. When eliminating a ritual is too difficult, realize that some great exposure ideas can result from thinking of the other ways that you can challenge your OCD rituals. Delaying a ritual by waiting 5 extra minutes before washing your hands, or changing a ritual like removing a line from an OCD ritualized prayer, or putting a limit on a ritual like only washing my hands 4x in a row instead of 5x in a row, are all great ways to fill your Fear Hierarchy with exposures that are gradual, iterative steps towards completely eliminating your rituals.

Walk Away: Does your OCD wants you to do things in certain ways at certain times? Try taking a different physical route through your routine to challenge OCD. Maybe when you use the bathroom at work, your OCD wants you to wash your hands once in the bathroom and then stop at the kitchen sink and wash a second time before you return to your desk. Try taking a different route back to your desk so that you don't have to pass the kitchen anymore.

Set ERP-Style Goals: ERP is going to be an entirely new mindset, not just because you have OCD, but because you're a human being and we all naturally try and avoid discomfort in certain areas of our life. Getting into the ERP mindset involves setting a whole new set of goals for yourself. These are tough goals to implement, but if you truly incorporate them into your exposures, and into your life as a whole, OCD will have nothing left with which to control you. Try some of these goals on for size:

- I'm going to get contaminated.

- I'm going to mess up and make mistakes.

- I'm going to make myself confused.

168

- I'm going to not know the answer.

- I'm going to feel not right.

- I'm going to feel uncertain.

- I'm going to create discomfort in my body.

- I'm going to make myself feel anxiety, annoyance, guilt, disgust, etc.

- I'm going to see how high I can make the uncomfortable feeling.

- I'm going to see how long I can make the uncomfortable feeling last.

- I'm going to see if I can make the uncomfortable thoughts and feelings never go away.

Setting these goals for yourself will naturally lead to endless exposures you can do. They might even lead you to discover other areas where you have been avoiding and ritualizing without even knowing it.

Use the ERP Brainstorm Assessment: You can use the ERP Brainstorm assessment from earlier in this chapter to help you with this task of identifying exposures. Here are the 2 ways that the assessment may be useful:

1. *Look at the list of "Things I'm Currently Trying to Avoid."* An easy way to come up with exposure ideas is to simply reverse these areas of avoidance. If you've identified "rusty metal" and "movies with violent imagery" as things you've been avoiding, you can write down "Touching rusty metal items" and "Watching movies with violent imagery" as potential exposures.

2. *Look at the list of rituals and corresponding triggers.* You can easily create exposures by combining 1) exposure to one of your triggers with 2) resisting the corresponding ritual. So, if you identify that you complete the ritual "erasing and rewriting my last sentence" every time you encounter the trigger "having a bad thought during homework," the exposure becomes "Think a bad thought during homework and resist erasing and rewriting." If you identify the ritual "calling and asking my wife for reassurance" every time you encounter the trigger "thinking I

might have hit someone on the way to work," the exposure becomes "thinking about all the bumps my car hit while driving to work without calling my wife and asking for reassurance"

Now go ahead and try and come up with as many general ideas for exposures as possible. Austin, who is struggling with scrupulosity concerns, identifies the following initial ideas for exposures:

- Looking at the number 666 and not praying
- Seeing someone with tattoos and piercings and not praying
- Holding a cross upside down

Jenna, who is struggling with contamination fears, identifies these ideas in her first round of brainstorming:

- Getting into her bed at night without taking a shower
- Allowing her sister into her room
- Allowing her Mom to put something out of place in her room.

Once these initial, general ideas are identified, it's time to start a second round of brainstorming. The goal of this second round is to expand on your initial ideas by creating multiple, gradual steps and also adding some variation.

Austin and Jenna challenge themselves to identify a variety of baby steps in the areas they have already identified.

Austin thinks some more about his praying and reveals some more details about his praying ritual. He notes that he has to say "I love you Jesus. And I reject Satan. I will try my absolute best, at all times, to follow your path and not stray towards the darkness." He also notes that he has to say these words with as much conviction and sincerity as possible. If he messes up the words while reciting it or doesn't think he had the proper conviction and sincerity, he will have to redo the prayer. With this additional information in mind, he is able to expand on his exposure list with the following ideas:

- Looking at the number 666 and not praying
    - Looking at the number 666 and praying without the last part of my prayer
    - Writing out the number 666 and praying without the last part of my prayer
    - Writing out 2 sixes and praying without the first part of my prayer
    - Saying the number 6 out loud and praying without the "I reject Satan" part
    - Watching a scene from a horror movie and not praying afterwards
    - Not redoing prayer if sincerity is "off"
- Seeing someone with tattoos and piercings and not praying
    - Looking up pictures of "tattoo fails" online and saying only part of my prayer afterwards
    - Looking at pictures of Christian tattoos online and not praying afterwards
    - Staring at my mother's pierced ears and not praying afterwards
    - Staring at my mother's pierced ears and saying the number 6 out loud
    - Looking up pictures of extreme piercings online and not praying perfectly afterwards

171

- o Going to the 6th page of the bible and reading what is written

- o Reading page 66 of the bible

- o Reading page 666 of the bible

- Holding a cross upside down

  - o Drawing an upside down cross and then "fixing" it after 30 seconds

  - o Drawing an upside down cross and then "fixing" it after 30 minutes

  - o Drawing an upside down cross and then keeping it in his pocket all day

As you can see, the number of possible exposures can become limitless once you start getting into the details of your rituals and start creatively playing with the variety. Jenna, who is struggling with the contamination fears, primarily around her bedroom, expands upon her list with the following additions:

- Getting into her bed at night without taking a shower

  - o Leaving an item of dirty laundry on my bed all day

  - o Showering but wearing the same pajamas 2 days in a row

  - o Not changing my sheets for 2 weeks

  - o Going downstairs and sitting in the living room for 30 minutes between showering and getting into bed

- Allowing her sister into her room

  - o Having a conversation with my sister while she stands in the doorway to my bedroom

  - o Allowing my sister to step 10 feet into my room, stand there for 1 minute and then leave

- o Allowing my sister to stand in my room for 15 minutes
- o Playing a board game with my sister on the floor of my bedroom
- o Allowing my sister to sit on my bed for 15 minutes, at the bottom with the bedspread on

- Allowing her Mom to put something out of place in her room
  - o Allowing my mom to be in my room for 5 minutes
  - o Allowing my mom to be in my room and look at the items on my dresser without touching anything
  - o Allowing my mom to touch the items on my dresser without moving them
  - o Allowing my mom to move some of the items on my dresser and leave them that way for 1 hour
  - o Allowing mom to move an item in my room to a completely different location and leaving it there indefinitely

Now for your turn, go ahead and brainstorm away, and come up with as many exposure ideas as you can. If you really want to go to town, it's not unheard of to have a fear hierarchy with 100 items or more (depending on the obsession and how elaborate the rituals). If you get stuck, just come back to that initial question: What is currently difficult to do?

A Few Ideas to Get You Started

If you're struggling to identify and design exposures to challenge your obsessions, here are some tried and true ideas to get you started.

Reading Triggering Words and Phrases Off of Index Cards: This is basically OCD exposure therapy in its purest form. You are going straight for the words and thoughts that trigger your fears. Write down some words or phrases related to your obsession on a bunch of index cards and read them out loud to yourself or someone else. Here are some examples of things you can write on index cards:

- *Triggering Words:* Names of different viruses, synonyms for throw up, violent words, words around pedophilia and children, triggering religious or sacrilegious words, names of people you think are "emotionally contaminated" etc.

- *Triggering Thoughts:* I'm a violent person, I'm going to kill someone some day and end up in prison, I'm going to hell, I'm a sinner, I like little children, I left the stove on at home, my house is burning down as we speak, I have an awful memory, I can't be trusted, I don't really have OCD, my fears are actually real, etc.

Writing and Reciting a Triggering Story: No more avoiding your feared scenario. Go ahead and tell a story about your fears coming true. And don't be afraid to use as much detail as possible, just to make sure you're not avoiding parts of the scenario. How exactly are you going to go about your shooting spree? What steps are you going to take when you sell your soul to the devil? Remember, OCD is controlling you because of your unwillingness to think these thoughts. The only way to get your life back from OCD is to stop being afraid to have the thoughts, no matter how disturbing, upsetting, or "unlike you" they may be. As you write your story, be sure that it's written in the "I" rather than "he" or "she." You should be the center of the story. Also, make sure you don't go over the top and create a story that's not believable. You want the story to capture your feared scenario in the realistic way you fear it could actually occur.

Recording Yourself Saying Triggering Words, Statements, or a Story and then Play it Back on Repeat: This one is an extension of the first 2 suggestions with a little more intensity. You'll have to first find a free app for your phone that can record your voice and then play it back on a loop. This time, go ahead and record yourself saying the triggering words, thoughts, statements, or stories, and then play it back to yourself on repeat. Spoiler alert: The way this exposure usually works is you're triggered at first, and eventually become bored. Also keep in mind that this can be a double exposure if you become annoyed or embarrassed by the sound of your voice. If you feel up for this second exposure, take the opportunity to tolerate and accept the way your voice sounds on the recording.

Watching Triggering Media: The Internet age has brought us a wealth of exposures at our fingertips. Whatever your triggering topic may be, you will find abundant videos, pictures, and text on that topic. To identify exposures, simply think about what you DON'T want to see, hear, or read about and identify gradual exposure steps you can complete. If you're struggling with a fear of throwing up, you won't suffer from a lack of throw up videos online. For harm fears, review the psychological profile of a serial killer and see how many of the characteristics you fit (while resisting your reassurance rituals). For contamination concerns, you can pull up microscopic imagery of germs. This all, of course, comes with the caveat that there are things on the internet no one should ever see. When it comes to violent and sexual images, take care to protect yourself from traumatizing content.

Writing Exposure Scripts: Exposure scripts are a great way to target your obsession in a very personalized and focused way. You create a narrative that specifically reminds you of the areas of uncertainty that you need to accept as well as the futility of trying to use rituals to remove this certainty. You then complete the script with a statement about why you are going to commit to resisting your rituals. Exposure scripts take some time to write, but once you have one or two written you have an easy daily exposure you can do from almost anywhere. Here are some examples that you can fashion your own scripts after.

Script 1: Contamination OCD

I can never be absolutely certain that my hands are clean. Germs can be anywhere. Some are completely harmless. Some could get me a little bit sick with a cold or flu. Some could even be contaminated with serious and deadly illnesses and diseases. There is no way for me to know with absolute certainty what items in the world might be contaminated with these germs. There is no test I can carry with me to test every surface I come into contact with. There is just no way to know.

Even if I wash my hands all day, every day, I can still become contaminated the second I finish washing my hands. I could even breathe in a dangerous germ. Even if I ask my parents or others around me if my hands are clean, they might not know. Even if they tell me I'm fine, they still might be wrong. The truth is that my OCD wants me to achieve something that's not possible. No number of rituals will ever give me the certainty I'm looking for. I have to accept uncertainty. I have to accept that there will always be risk in life.

I'm going to commit to telling my OCD that it's right, and that I might be contaminated" and I'm going to resist completing my rituals anyway. I know that this will be extremely difficult at first, but if I stick with it, it will get easier, and I will get my life back.

Script 2: Health-Related OCD

I can never be completely certain that there's nothing seriously wrong with my health. And I can never be certain about how long I'll live. I can't be sure that I'll always be there with Lucy, and that she'll have a mom growing up. I could be in a car accident that kills me tomorrow. I could develop a cancer that kills me before I'm ready. Or I could live a long and healthy life beyond what I'm expecting. I can't read the future, and there's no way to know any of these things for certain.

Even if I go to the doctor for checkups, I could develop a cancer that spreads quickly between visits. Doctors and instruments could miss something that's seriously wrong with me. Even if I read about health issues online, I could still be unaware of something that's happening inside my body that's not symptomatic yet.

I want to stop completing excessive rituals around my health. I want to stop focusing on the future and enjoy the present. And if I continue to worry about health issues all of the time, I won't be able to enjoy life. I'm going to accept the inevitable uncertainty around my health and accept that there will always be health risks in life no matter how many rituals I do. I know that if I can resist my rituals, it will be hard at first, but it will get easier with time.

Script 3: Fear I Don't Love My Fiancé

I can never be 100% completely sure that I love Jason. I might just think I love him, when deep down I really don't. It's possible that, for the past 5 years, I could have convinced myself that I love him and made myself feel things that I wouldn't have otherwise felt. Maybe I'm just in love with the idea of Jason, and not the actual person Jason. Maybe, I just really want to be married, and I'm ignoring the negative feelings I harbor towards Jason.

The fact is that there's no way to completely prove to my OCD that I'm in love with Jason. There's just no way to prove, without a doubt, that I'm feeling an emotion, and why I'm feeling that emotion. Even if I avoid any negative thoughts about our relationship, even if I recount all the happy moments, even if I think about every detail of our relationship for the rest of my life, I will still never be able to prove to OCD that I love Jason.

I'm going to stop avoiding my intrusive thoughts like "I don't love Jason" or "I hate Jason." I'm going to stop acting like I'm afraid of these thoughts, and that I can't handle them. I'm going to have these thoughts on purpose when I'm able. I know that if I continue to face these thoughts, I will be less triggered by them, and change my relationship with them. And I will take my life back from OCD.

Some More Exposure Ideas, by Obsession

Here are a few more specific ideas to help you get into the exposure mindset. Just remember that you are always thinking of ways to move directly towards your anxiety and actually do the things your OCD is telling you not to do:

Fear of Throwing Up

- View videos and pictures of vomit and people vomiting
- Describe what it feels like to get an upset stomach
- Make a list of synonyms for vomit, and read them
- Do something to cause stomach sensations/nausea (Spin in an office chair, exercising after eating, make yourself full)
- Kneel over a toilet and spit into it

Social Anxiety / Social Fears

- Attend a lecture and ask a question
- Ask a question during a work meeting
- Knock something over in a store
- Say hi to a salesclerk
- Text a friend
- Wear an item of clothing that really stands out and draws attention to you
- Ask a stranger for the time

178

- Give an opinion to someone

- Say 'Hi' to a cashier

Panic Fears

- Breathing exposures (you may want to do these with someone supervising or nearby first). Hold your breath for a certain amount of time, hyperventilate (i.e., rapidly breathe in and out) on purpose for a certain amount of time, breathe through a thin coffee straw for a certain amount of time

- Spin in a chair

- Put your head upside down between your legs for 10 seconds. Quickly lift your head and hold it up for 10 seconds. Repeat

- Shake your head from side to side for 10 seconds. Stop for 10 seconds. Repeat

- Wear something like a scarf or necktie tightly around your neck for 1 minute then take a break. Repeat

- Run up and down a set of stairs until you can feel your heart racing

- Stare at a light for 10 seconds and try and read something immediately after

- Find some optical illusions online and stare at them until your vision blurs or you start to experience derealization (feeling distant from your body and/or reality)

- Stare at your hand until you start to experience derealization

Scrupulosity Fears

- Say a prayer the "wrong" way

- Say or write something sacrilegious

- Watch a triggering horror movie scene

179

- Read a book or story on witchcraft or satanism
- Write a story about sinning and going to hell
- Write a random word (graffiti) in a library book
- Leave a candy wrapper (litter) in a public building
- Omit something at confession
- Don't apologize
- Watch a comedy routine or movie scene about a taboo subject

Contamination

- Touch contaminated surfaces/items for increasingly longer periods of time
- Inhale near a triggering area or substance
- Work up to being fully contaminated, eventually wiping contamination around your entire body
- Pick up cigarette butts and garbage with your bare hands
- Put your shoes on your bed
- Handle raw meat
- Touch a toilet seat

Pedophile OCD

- Take a seat within view of a children's park and (discreetly of course) say or think to yourself "I like little kids" every 30 seconds while keeping your eyes on the children
- Pull up an article describing the characteristics of a pedophile and identify all the similarities between you and the profile
- Write a story about how you would carry out the abduction of a child
- Go to a destination for kids (like a pumpkin patch) and walk around, identifying in your mind which children you're most attracted to

180

Fear That Your Thoughts Have Power

- Stand within sight of a road with traffic. With every car that passes, look at it and whisper "crash"

- Watch pedestrians on a sidewalk. Quietly whisper to yourself or think "trip" as each person passes

- Write down a prediction on a piece of paper. 'I'm going to break a bone today' or 'My mom's going to get a flat tire today.' Adding a specific timeframe like 'today' helps you see if your thoughts end up making anything happen or not

Harm OCD

- Leave a shoe in the middle of the floor where someone might trip over it

- Carry around a pocketknife (where this is legal and acceptable)

- Allow yourself to experience being angry and upset with others

- Read stories about real people who have "snapped"

- Writing a story about how you will "snap" and kill someone in the future

- Walk around with a piece of paper in your pocket that says "I want to kill"

- Hold rope, a knife, or mediation without supervision

Just Right OCD

- Wear an uncomfortable item of clothing or wear an item of clothing the "wrong" way

- Step through doorways the "wrong" way or along a sidewalk the "wrong" way

- Change the order of your morning or evening routine

- Touch something with one side of your body and don't even it out by touching it with the other side

- Tell a story the wrong way or let another person tell a story the wrong way without correcting them

- Let the food on your plate touch

- Allow someone to move things around in your room

- Do things at the "wrong" time

- Complete an activity you usually have to do "just right" (playing piano, doing your hair, speaking, etc.) and don't redo or fix things when it's not "just right"

- Move things to the "wrong" place

- Sit somewhere different at dinner

Ranking Your Exposures

You will have to decide on a ranking system to use for rating the difficulty of each of your exposures. After choosing a ranking system, you can then go through your list of exposures, and rate them one by one. Let's review some of the options so that you can find the one that works best for you.

Easy/Moderate/Difficult: For some people grouping exposures into 3 basic categories is sufficient. This method works when you don't feel that you need a lot of fine-toothed differentiation between your exposures. It can also be helpful for younger children who would find it easy to understand Red / Yellow / Green for ratings or a simple Thumbs up / Thumbs down / Thumbs sideways.

The 1-10 Distress Score: This is probably the most common ranking system. You rank your exposures based on the emotional distress you anticipate experiencing during the exposure. 1 is almost no distress whatsoever and 10 is unbearable, panic-attack-level distress. You would base the score based on the specific emotion you will be experiencing during the exposure, whether that be anxiety or another emotion like anger, disgust or shame. When using this scale, helpful and therapeutic exposures tend to be in the 4-6 range of distress. This indicates that they are not too difficult but not too easy.

The 1-100 Distress Score (sometimes called the SUDS scale for Subjective Units of Discomfort): This is the same premise as the 1-10 scale but is for those who like a little more differentiation between their exposures and some more detailed reporting during the habituation process. If you find yourself trying the 1-10 scale and wanting to use 3.5 or 5.25 a lot, this may be the better scale for you.

Yes/Maybe/No: This is a method based on how willing you are to complete the exposures. Those items you're willing to do get a 'Yes.' Items you're not quite sure about get a 'Maybe." And those exposures you are absolutely not going to do (yet!) get a 'No.'

The 1-10 Willingness Score: Just like the Yes/Maybe/No Scale but with some more differentiation. These willingness scales are ideal for those who have a hard time predicting what their emotional response will be during an exposure but who can easily identify their current willingness to do an exposure.

Exercise: Completing Your Fear Hierarchy

Once you have a list of exposures and have attributed a rating to each one, it's time to finalize your fear hierarchy. You can use the hierarchy included on the next page. Keep in mind that your hierarchy is going to be a living document. This is just your first draft. Once you start exposures you may find the actual difficulty of some exposures will turn out to be easier or harder than you expected. That's fine and in fact, totally normal. You will also inevitably come up with new exposure ideas as you progress. And probably most exciting is the fact that as you master exposures and find them to be no longer triggering or worth doing, you can put a line straight through them and cross them off the list.

On the next 2 pages, you'll see an initial fear hierarchy created by Ella, a 10-year-old girl who is struggling with fears of getting sick from allowing germs to enter her mouth. With the help of her parents, she created the initial fear ladder. You will notice there is still room for the fear hierarchy to be expanded even further. An exposure like "give Dad a hug" for example could be gradually increased in terms of length of time or closeness of the hug. When Ella begins the exposure process, the fear ladder will inevitably evolve as she discovers how easy or hard the exposures actually are in practice, and she continues to think of new exposures to add. She also will cross off exposures once they are no longer triggering.

Following Ella's fear hierarchy, there is a blank hierarchy for you to create one for yourself.

FEAR HIERARCHY

Obsessions (fear themes targeted by these exposures)	Ritual Prevention (rituals to resist during exposures)
FEAR OF GETTING SICK FROM CONTACT WITH GERMS FEAR OF SAYING THE WRONG THING FEAR OF MAKING A MISTAKE	KEEP ARMS/HANDS IN A NATURAL POSITION (INSTEAD OF EXTENDED FAR FROM MY BODY AND FACE BREATHE NORMALLY THROUGH BOTH MY NOSE AND MOUTH

Difficulty	Exposure
10	EAT POTATO CHIPS, LICK FINGERS EVERY BITE / NO HANDWASH BEFORE OR AFTER
10	SHARE MEAL WITH MOM AND DAD USING SAME PLATE AND UTENSILS AS THEM
10	NO LONGER KEEP TOOTHBRUSH WRAPPED IN PLASTIC BAG
10	USE SILVERWARE FROM THE HOUSE INSTEAD OF INDIVIDUALLY WRAPPED PLASTIC UTENSILS
10	RUB BOTH OF MY HANDS ALL OVER MY FACE / NO HANDWASH AFTER
9	LIMIT HANDWASHING TO AFTER BATHROOM USE AND BEFORE MEALS
9	GIVING MOM A KISS ON THE LIPS
9	HOLD DOORKNOB UNTIL HABITUATING / NO HANDWASH AFTERWARDS
8	HAVING SOMEONE TAKE A SIP OF MY WATER BEFORE I DRINK IT
8	EAT 3 BITES OF A SNACK FROM A BAG THAT WAS FIRST OPENED DAYS AGO
8	LEAVE DINNER OUT ON MY PLATE FOR 60 MINUTES BEFORE EATING IT
8	EAT ONE BITE OF A SNACK FROM A BAG THAT WAS FIRST OPENED DAYS AGO
8	EAT FULL MEAL OF LEFTOVERS
8	TOUCH A FINGER BRIEFLY TO MY LIPS

185

FEAR HIERARCHY

Difficulty	Exposure
8	HOLD DOORKNOB FOR 10 MINS W/ BOTH HANDS / WAIT 60 MINS BEFORE WASHING HANDS
8	WASH MY FACE AS PART OF MY NIGHTLY ROUTINE
8	HOLD HANDS WITH MY MOM / WAIT TO WASH HANDS FOR 20 MINUTES
7	TELL A STORY OF A RECENT EVENT TO MY AUNT / SPEAK RAPIDLY / DON'T START OVER
7	HOLD HAND ON MY CHEEK FOR 10 MINS / NO HAND WASH FOR 10 MINS AFTERWARDS
7	HOLD DOORKNOB FOR 10 MINS W BOTH HANDS / WAIT 10 MINS BEFORE WASHING HANDS
7	GIVE DAD A HUG
7	PURPOSEFULLY MAKE A MISTAKE ON HOMEWORK
7	PLACE MY UTENSIL ON THE TABLE BETWEEN BITES
7	USE THE TV REMOTE / WAIT TO WASH HANDS FOR 20 MINS
6	EAT 3 BITES OF LEFTOVERS
6	RECITE ALPHABET RAP (FOUND ONLINE) AS QUICKLY AS POSSIBLE WITHOUT REDOING MISTAKES
6	LEAVE DINNER OUT FOR 15 MINUTES BEFORE STARTING TO EAT IT
5	BRIEFLY TOUCH A DOORKNOB W/O MY SHIRT AS A BARRIER / NO HAND WASH FOR 10 MINS
5	ONLY WASH UNDER FINGERNAILS ONCE BRIEFLY WHILE WASHING HANDS
5	EAT SNACK FOOD WITH HANDS FROM FRESHLY OPENED BAG
5	USE THE SAME PLASTIC FORK FOR 2 MEALS WITHOUT THROWING IT OUT
4	BRIEFLY TOUCH MY HAND TO MY CHEEK / NO HANDWASH FOR 5 MINUTES
3	SAY "I'M NOT SORRY" EVERY TIME I SAY AN EXCESSIVE "SORRY"
3	DON'T ASK OTHERS IF THIS IS MY GLASS DURING MEALS

FEAR HIERARCHY

Obsessions (fear themes targeted by these exposures)

Ritual Prevention (rituals to resist during exposures)

Difficulty	Exposure

Available for download at *https://pittsburghocdtreatment.com/publications/the-ocd-travel-guide/*

FEAR HIERARCHY

Difficulty	Exposure

Available for download at *https://pittsburghocdtreatment.com/publications/the-ocd-travel-guide/*

Step 5: Beginning Exposures

With all of the pieces in place, all that's left is to begin the exposure process. It's important that you set yourself up for success by setting aside a daily exposure time. Some exposures will of course have to occur during specific times of day (exposures around morning routine or mealtimes, for example) but other exposures you may be able to implement any time of day. In the latter case, make sure to plan exposures around any responsibilities. Also consider when during the day you feel best prepared to deal with the emotional discomfort of exposures, and when you will have sufficient time to sit through the discomfort without ritualizing. Once, you've selected a time, you're ready to get started.

Here are the basic elements of an exposure:

1. **Exposure to your trigger:** Pick something from the fear hierarchy and do it!

2. **Thoughts and feelings show up:** Get ready to experience a feeling of being in danger, a sense that something is not right, an unsettling feeling of uncertainty, and/or an urge to stop what you are doing and fix the situation/

3. **Resist the urge to engage in rituals:** Accept the fear, uncertainty, risk, and discomfort/

4. **Sit with the thoughts and feelings until they subside**

As you prepare to select exposures from your fear hierarchy and get started, here are some additional considerations to set yourself up for success:

Start with the Easy Stuff: Initially, the most important experiences that you want to have with exposure therapy are any experiences that make you feel successful with the treatment. When you're first starting exposure therapy, take care not to pick an exposure that's too hard and leaves you ritualizing for days. Start with exposures you feel confident about successfully completing.

You Don't Have to do the REALLY Hard Exposures: The most important part of exposures, believe it or not, isn't seeing how much you can trigger yourself. It's actually seeing how thoroughly you can resist your rituals and stay in the exposure. If you choose a 7 out of 10 difficulty exposure and partly ritualize through it, this is way less therapeutic than choosing a 3 out of 10 difficulty exposure that allows you to completely resist all of your physical and mental rituals throughout the entire exposure. Don't forget that your rituals are the problem perpetuating your OCD. And that changing your behavior, and not ritualizing, is the number one thing you can do to start showing your OCD who's boss.

And all that being said, if you can do a difficult exposure without ritualizing, by all means, go for it. The more intense the experience, as long as you can resist those rituals, the more of an impact it will have on that pesky fear that's stuck in your head.

Think of This as Your Mental Health Workout: Completing exposures is hard work, but it's also nothing you can't handle. You might want to think of your exposures as a workout for your mental health. Just like someone training for a marathon is going to have to deal with burning lungs, exhausted muscles, and a pounding heart rate in their quest to achieve their goal, you're going to have to accept the discomfort that comes with your exposures on the path towards reaching your own life goals. The old adage 'No pain, no gain' is highly appropriate here. And just like the person training for the marathon (who won't run 26.2 miles in the first week of training), you should plan to start small and gradually increase the exposure difficulty too.

Mix Things Up: It is highly probable that you are struggling with more than one obsession. But don't feel like you need to keep the various parts of your OCD separate from one another. In fact, it can be quite therapeutic to mix together the various rituals and obsessions you are experiencing into one fear hierarchy and vary the obsessions you are targeting with your exposures. The reason for this is that you ultimately want to view all of your obsessions as variations of the same thing. They are all related to a fear of uncertainty, an avoidance of discomfort, and a perceived need to control your thoughts and your feelings. The particulars of your obsessions can be somewhat of a distraction from the bigger issue. Mixing things up can help you focus your attention on the larger issue at hand, and not get too focused on the specific content of your obsessional themes.

The More, The Better: At intensive treatment programs for OCD, the standard expectation is that you're doing 20+ exposures a day. While you may not have the time, ability, or need to be doing that many yourself, it still holds true that the more exposures you do, the more results you can expect to see.

Repeat, Repeat, Repeat: As you work through your fear hierarchy, the ultimate triumph comes from crossing exposures off that list because they are no longer triggering you. But it can take a fair amount of repetition for you to get to that point. As you implement a new exposure, track your emotional response to the exposure over time. The more you repeat, the lower you can expect that response to get. And you don't have to stop with repeating the exposure daily. Sometimes, the best thing to do is repeat an exposure 3, 4, or 5 times back-to-back in the same exposure session. See how low you can get that emotional response over time. Down to 2 out of 10? Down to a 1 out of 10? Down to the point when you're completely bored with it?

Also, keep in mind that many exposures will actually become part of a new way of living that you introduce into your life for good. If you identified "only writing my class notes once" as an exposure because you've been rewriting all of your class notes 2 times each evening, this is also going to be a healthy life goal that you're going to want to keep in place.

Mess Up. It's Okay: Allow yourself to have a bad exposure day every so often. It's okay if you're having an off day when you just feel overly triggered by everything and can't seem to resist all of your rituals. This is just part of the process. And messing up, taking the bad with the good, having good and bad days; these things are all part of the process of challenging your OCD.

191

Now, with all of that out of the way, it's time for you to get started. Go ahead and find the time and place and start exposures!

Fine Tuning Exposures

Your ERP time is going to be your laboratory and your exposures are going to be your experiments. There will always be some trial and error in this process. When something isn't working, don't be too quick to give up on it. Sometimes problems with ERP can be corrected with a quick fix. Here are some tips and recommendations for how to address some common problems.

Obsessions with Certain Mental Habits: If you are engaged in one of the following (or similar) mental behaviors, you may have to take a slightly different approach:

- Habitually "noticing" (or hyper focusing on) your bodily functions, such as breathing, blinking, heart rate, etc.

- Habitually counting things in your surroundings (the sides of pictures, the corners of tables, the number of objects on the shelf)

You may be tempted to think that your exposures should involve focusing more attention on these things you're already doing all the time (i.e., focusing even more on your breathing and counting things even more), but this would actually be misguided. The problem you are experiencing is actually TOO much preoccupation with certain brain habits. You have developed a habit of "noticing your bodily functions." Or your brain has fallen into an almost automatic, compulsive habit of counting things. Your obsession, or feared scenario, in these situations is usually that you will never be able to stop these things from happening. You will notice you bodily functions, or count everything you see for the rest of your life. It's this thought that is causing the anxiety. In these situations, you need to 1) learn some strategies for interrupting the habit you don't like, but you also need to 2) be less upset every time you fall into the habit. Here are a couple of strategies to use when faced with these obsessions:

192

1. *Accept your habit:* First and foremost, realize that the thing you are actually afraid of is the fact that you might never be able to stop focusing your attention on these things. And because this is the thing that distresses you, your exposure is thinking about the fact that this might be true. Exposures will involve accepting the fact that you might continue to notice and focus on these things to varying degrees for the rest of your life. You might be paying attention to your blinking during your wedding. You might be aware of your breathing during the birth of your children. You might be counting everything in the room on your deathbed. Realize that this isn't the worst thing in the world, and that you can handle continuing to notice these things. Through exposing yourself to these possibilities and accepting them, you will gradually reduce your distress. And, when you're not bothered by these habits as much as you are now, that is when you will actually start to focus less on your body's mundane functions. You can get better at catching yourself "over focusing" or counting and stopping yourself. But just remember that you WILL continue to fall into these habits, and ACCEPTING that and caring less about that will go a long way towards managing your anxiety.

2. *Choose what you pay attention to:* Also realize that you do have some control over what you pay attention to, and that when you catch yourself noticing body functions or notice your brain counting, you can do something about it. Your greatest ally in this situation is the scientific fact that your brain can only pay attention to one thing at a time. When you catch yourself paying attention to your breath, or counting things, you need to accept the fact that you were doing it again (don't let yourself get frustrated and angry about it. It's totally okay that you were doing it), and then simply direct your attention towards something else. Here are some alternate targets for your attention that you can introduce:

   • For hyper focusing on your bodily sensations, point your focus towards something other than your body. Pay attention to things in your environment. If you're on a hike, notice the sound of the birds,

193

the color of the leaves, see how many different species of trees, shrubs and plants you can find. If you are indoors, look at some of the details in your surroundings. Are there things you've never noticed before? Use your sense of sight, hearing, smell, and touch. See what you can discover. Focus on the lyrics of the song you're listening to, the emotional state of the characters in the movie you're watching, the ideas that someone talking to you is trying to express.

- For habitual counting compulsions that seem to happen automatically, it's time to set your mind to noticing things about your environment other than how many sides all the shapes in the room have. Those sides of that frame your mind is counting over and over again? How about focusing on the painting it's holding. How do you feel about the color combination? How does the painting make you feel? Is it abstract? Realistic? Do you like the painting? And the features of that person's face that your mind won't stop counting? How about listening to their words and trying as best you can to "get" exactly what they are trying to express. And what do you think about their face? Attractive? Symmetrical? Not so much? What emotions do you think they are feeling? Hopefully you're getting the point. Counting is simply one of many thinking activities that your mind can busy itself with. Practice trying out some of the other things you can think about when you're interacting with your surroundings.

Trying to Answer Unanswerable Questions: Another obsession that can lead to primarily mental rituals is a preoccupation with existential concerns or other unanswerable questions. Will you ever find out if life is real (and you're not in the *Matrix* world or in a dream)? Will you ever perfectly know who you are (and the corresponding question will you be able to live fully in-line with your real self)? Will you ever fully know how other people are perceiving you? Or the myriad number of other existential concerns you could ponder? Keep in mind that the exposure in these situations becomes accepting that your mental activity is futile and that you will never be able to satisfactorily answer these questions. Sometimes, labeling these questions as unanswerable can effectively suck the air out of your motivation to keep thinking about them. You then are left to accept the uncertainty and practice directing your attention towards better uses of your mental energy.

Is Distraction Okay? In general, when you introduce distraction into an exposure, you neutralize the efficacy of the exposure. The goal of an exposure is to focus on your feared thoughts, experience the wave of emotion that they bring, and hang out while the thoughts and feelings pass. So, in general, the answer to this question is, no, distraction is not okay. In a pure exposure you shouldn't be introducing coping skills, you shouldn't be focusing on other things, you shouldn't even be practicing breathing exercises to try and calm yourself down. The goal is to realize that your thoughts and feelings pass all on their own, without any action needed from you.

That being said, if you find yourself in an exposure that triggered you more than you expected and you're just overwhelmed by discomfort to the point that you can't even process the experience, using a distraction or coping skill is better than using rituals. A distraction or coping skill may neutralize the exposure, but it won't make your OCD worse. Rituals, on the other hand will reinforce your fears and further entrench you in the OCD Cycle of Avoidance.

Lastly, when a mental ritual is particularly strong, you can end up getting stuck in your head, and uncontrollably reviewing things over and over again. Simply exposing you to the thoughts and feelings and asking yourself to "stop" doing the mental ritual may be a pretty tall order. In these cases, you may have to identify a behavior to "start" doing to replace the mental activity you are trying to "stop" doing. Introducing tactile and sensory activities into the exposure (particularly something that gets you focused on a small goal) can really get you out of your head and focused on a task. This isn't distraction, per se, because you have to introduce the activity to interrupt the ritual. As you get better at doing things other than your mental ritual, however, you may find that you can even remove the alternate task and the motivation to engage in the habitual mental ritual has dissipated.

Do I Focus on 'What's Important' (i.e., My Values) During an Exposure? The START method presented in Chapter 4 introduced you to a holistic approach for living a healthy and full life as someone with OCD. This method helps you direct your attention towards something in life more important than your OCD thoughts and feelings. And it's the strategy to use when you are trying to study for a test or attend a family reunion or start practicing your guitar again or cooking dinner. However, planned exposures during your "exposure time" is a slightly different story. Your "exposure time" is your time to direct your attention directly at your OCD thoughts and feelings. Planned exposures are the focused, intensive part of your treatment intended to desensitize you to your thoughts and feelings by having you focus on them and experience them. So, sure. Momentarily remind yourself that you really want to go back to college and that's why you're doing ERP, but then direct your attention right back to the fear you might die of botulism from that can of food you're eating for your exposure.

What if I Don't Habituate? At the end of Chapter 2, we mentioned that there are 3 general trends when it comes to habituating to OCD thoughts and feelings. 1) You might habituate during an exposure (your anxiety lowers while you are still touching the contaminated object, for example), 2) you might habituate between exposures (your discomfort stays the same during the exposure but you notice that the exposure becomes gradually easier the more times you do it), or 3) you notice your tolerance for the discomfort increasing the more you do the exposure (the trigger stubbornly continues to make you feel the emotion but the more you practice feeling the emotion, the more willing you are to do things that cause you to feel that emotion). As you progress with exposures, figure out what type of habituation you are experiencing and adjust your expectations accordingly.

After the Exposure: What you do after an exposure can be just as important as what happens during the exposure. ERP is a learning treatment. You are giving your brain intense experiences and it is important that you both a) take care of yourself and b) don't do things that neutralize the experience. Feel free to do something relaxing, and to even reward yourself, after completing difficult exposures. But you should also have a plan for how to handle ritual urges after an exposure. You want to be careful not to erase the progress you are making with your exposures by completely ritualizing. For example, doing exposures in school might all be neutralized if you take a shower every day as soon as you get home. This is not to say that you have to resist all rituals after doing exposures, but you should at least limit, delay, change, or reduce any rituals you may do following an exposure. And you'll also want to keep your focus on the goal of eventually resisting all rituals throughout the day.

The 'Do I Want to Do This Exposure' Ritual: One of OCD's sneakier tricks is to get you habitually engaging in a ritual of figuring out whether you want to do an exposure or not. You may not identify this as a ritual because you haven't even started the exposure yet. But it is definitely a ritual, and one that has thwarted many an ERP participant. If you find yourself asking this question, going back and forth in your mind, and ultimately not doing the exposure, it's time to identify this as one of your rituals. You will have to get better at noticing the thought "Should I do this ritual?" when it pops into your head and committing yourself to not engaging with the question. Simply choose an exposure and move forward without getting lost in thought.

Getting Bothered by Being Bothered: You may notice, as you progress through the exposure process that your original obsessive thought fades, but the emotions remain. You very clearly can say with confidence "I'm probably not a twisted serial killer" or "I'm pretty sure I'm a heterosexual." Logically, you no longer have any difficulty combatting the thoughts, and yet you can't stop getting emotionally triggered whenever you encounter the name "Ted Bundy" or a rainbow flag. This can be incredibly frustrating on a number of levels. One you're now very clearly stuck with a fear you no longer want and, two, in the case of your sexuality fear, it can make you feel like you have some sort of prejudice towards people of a different sexuality. In these cases, you have to accept the existence of the unwanted emotional response to the trigger. It doesn't mean you haven't come a long way in treatment. You have. And it's okay that your brain is still having an irrational response to the world. As much as you may want your brain's fears to completely align with logic and reality, don't forget that you have OCD. It's a real thing. Many, many people have it. And it just means your life will always be a little different than

197

people without OCD. Lastly, it doesn't mean that you're prejudiced that you still get anxious whenever you see that rainbow flag. That's just a lingering OCD emotion. OCD is random. And your OCD fears don't represent you.

Some Common Mindset Problems During ERP: Be on the lookout for these common barriers to successfully engaging in ERP:

I'm doing this for others (i.e., my parents, my spouse, etc.): If your motivation is coming completely from others right now, you're probably going to have limited success at ERP. You may have to have a conversation with this other person (or discuss the situation with your therapist if you're in treatment) and let them know that your OCD treatment is becoming too much about them. Create some distance in your mind from this person and allow yourself to face your OCD one-on-one. Really ask yourself what is bothering you about OCD and start from that point. Maybe the things that are bothering you are different from what's bothering this person in your life, and this might lead to a completely different fear hierarchy. Let's face it, if you're reading this book, there is motivation there. It's just a matter of directing that motivation towards the things that are your current priorities.

I want to get better. But I want it to be quick and I want it to be easy: If you are feeling this way, it's time for an expectation adjustment. I've used this analogy elsewhere in this book, but ERP treatment is akin to training for a marathon. It is a big, difficult task, and there is no way around that. You wouldn't ask someone how to run a marathon without having to do all of the training. Likewise, you can't ask yourself how you are going to get a handle on your OCD without doing all the hard work. You have to face the reality of the task before you, mentally prepare yourself for difficult, hard work, and start each day ready to do something difficult. There is simply no other option.

I'm doing this, just so I don't have to have these thoughts and feelings anymore: While treatment works, and you can expect to eventually experience fewer distressing thoughts and feelings, having this as your goal as you move through treatment can be a real barrier to success. Progress in ERP can be very gradual, and so you're not always going to feel like you're having fewer uncomfortable thoughts and feelings. And the fear you have of your thoughts and feelings is actually serious fuel for your OCD. If you find yourself with this unhelpful goal, try an alternative goal. I'm going to get better at having thoughts and feeling feelings that I don't like. This sets you up for much less disappointment and frustration, and when you do notice things getting easier, it's just a nice surprise.

Resistance to success, feeling good, and feeling safe: OCD has probably trained you to think that anticipating danger is the preferred outlook on life. You may even find comfort in being alert, being anxious, worrying, and ritualizing. By engaging in ERP and challenging your OCD, you are taking steps to no longer live this way. It's not going to feel right, at first. It's going to feel weird, unsafe, and not right to try and stop worrying. But ultimately, you know deep down, that this is the life you are seeking for yourself. As you engage in exposures, you are going to have to be comfortable with the following things happening, because these things are ultimately the goals, and they are going to happen:

- Having positive thoughts about yourself

- Not worrying about future consequences

- Focusing on things other than danger, risk, discomfort, and uncertainty

- Disregarding your anxiety and other uncomfortable emotions

- Noticing evidence that you're fine and safe

- Doing things for fun

- Doing things for yourself (i.e., realizing you're worth your own focus and attention!)

- Not doing anything to fix something in the world

- Finding happiness and success, in OCD treatment and beyond

Reach for these goals and be ready for the flurry of negativity and pessimism that OCD will inevitably throw at you, and then keep having your positive thoughts and feelings anyway!

Chapter 6
Managing Your Brain During Your Travels

Your brain is possibly the single most important asset you are given at birth. A mass of billions of neurons, the number of tasks your brain is completing at any given time is unfathomable. And yet, your brain can also be your greatest curse. Many of the struggles associated with OCD come down to struggles you are having in your relationship with your brain. You are trying to get your brain to do one thing, and that stubborn organ in your head is doing another. Managing life with OCD, then, has to include a plan for how you're going to live with your brain.

You Are Not Your Brain. Your Brain Is Not You

There's an important distinction we need to make between "you" and "your brain," because they really are two different things. Think about it. If you and your brain were the same thing, how would you be able to do things like "notice" your thoughts, analyze your thoughts, and ask yourself if you agree with your thoughts? There is clearly a "you" separate from "your brain." Your brain is an organ, and just like other organs in your body, it performs a variety of functions without needing any input from "you." This even extends to the individual thoughts and feelings you might be having at any given point in time. So many of the mental experiences you have - the thoughts, the emotions, the urges, the memories, the worries - are not anything you decide to have. They just sort of happen. They are the product of that automatic part of your brain that is beyond your control. They are not "you." They are "your brain."

But this begs the question, if you are not your brain, then who are you? Well, the simple answer to that question is that you are something so much bigger than the random functions of your brain. YOU, the real you, the wise you, the observing you, is beyond the thoughts and emotions of the moment. YOU are the consciousness that has been there ever since you were first

200

born, observing the world through your senses, feeling your body's physical sensations, and experiencing your brain's thoughts and feelings. YOU are the constant. The YOU that is here right now reading this book is the same you that was peering out at the world at age 5 and 10. You've witnessed a few more things, have access to more information, and have refined your interests and beliefs over the years, but you're still the same consciousness. This real YOU is the decider in life. YOU get to choose how you want to behave in any given moment, how you want to live your life, and what things are most important to you. YOU get to set goals for yourself, whatever you want them to be. YOU get to choose what you value in life.

On the pages ahead, we'll be looking at the various functions of this crazy organ in your head we call your brain. And you'll be learning about how few of these functions are actually under your control. As you read ahead, challenge yourself to notice the real YOU that is separate from these various functions and remind yourself that YOU are not your brain.

Know When, and How, to Use Your Brain's Various Functions

Let's look at your brain in a bit more detail. Your brain has some very specific functions it's tasked with performing. And it works tirelessly to complete these duties. When you have OCD, it becomes extremely important to understand your brain, its functions, and what it can and can't do. This is because your OCD is constantly urging you to take control of some part of your brain that you can't control. OCD promises that if you try hard enough, you'll only feel these emotions, and never those emotions. It wants you to believe you'll eventually be able prevent certain thoughts from ever entering your mind again. Basically, it makes a whole lot of false promises. Knowing your brain's limits, then, is critical to staying on the route you've set for yourself. So, let's take a closer look at these various functions of your brain, discuss some of the important purposes they serve, and see how to appropriately manage them on your travels. After all, how you respond to your brain can have a major impact on whether you keep moving towards your goals or take the next exit from life.

201

Your Thought Generator

Your brain is a thought-generating machine. Morning until night, it is coming up with thoughts - the result of its tireless work trying to make connections and draw comparisons between things. And sort of like one of those Mad Libs books, the results that your brain's Thought Generator comes up with can be pretty zany at times. What if (*enter random scary event*) happens? What if I'm a (*enter an extremely disturbing type of person*)? Am I as good as (*name of peer or acquaintance*)? The true reason for this creative thought-generating app is that, believe it or not, your brain really wants you to survive. We homo sapiens have been incredibly successful as a species because of our brain's ability to come up with crazy ideas. What if the fish are in the same place they were yesterday morning? And what if I sharpened this stick into a spear to catch those fish? But what if that big bear is also lurking around that area? Notice how these 3 questions are all examples of the brain trying to guess at and predict things that aren't visible or in existence yet. They are the result of the brain's Thought Generator. And because this Thought Generator has been so integral to our survival, the brain pretty much keeps it running all the time in the background. Everything we see, everything anyone says, every memory that pops into our head; our brains are constantly observing and analyzing these occurrences, and then posing questions, drawing comparisons, making predictions, and trying to come up with even more creative possibilities. And it all happens without us needing to do anything. This is the Thought Generator doing its thing. Let's look at some general guidelines for how you can effectively live with this Thought Generator in your head without getting totally derailed in life.

Don't Take It Personally That Your Brain Came Up with A Disturbing or Taboo or Un-PC Thought: Just because your brain comes up with a thought, that doesn't say anything about YOU. Your brain finds material for thoughts in all sorts of places: movies, the news, things you've heard other people say. And, as mentioned, your brain is incredibly creative and can come up with crazy things you've never even encountered before. Oh, and also keep in mind that your Thought Generator does not come equipped with a filter, and it does not care about societal norms and taboos. Anything and everything is game when it comes to your brain's creative impulse. And if you fight your brain in this area, if you start trying to make your brain NOT have certain thoughts, you will only become more consumed by those thoughts. Just realize they are just thoughts. They're not good or bad. And they don't say anything about you other than the fact that you have a brain, and brains come up with thoughts.

Don't Engage with Thoughts That Aren't Helpful to You. Just because a though disturbs you and/or makes you anxious, this doesn't mean that the thought is important and worth your time. The stronger your behavioral reaction to a message, the more likely your brain is to keep reminding you of that thought. So, if your brain sends you a random message, and you spend an hour arguing back and forth with your brain, your brain will take that as proof that the initial message was really important and something it needs to keep reminding you about. On the other hand, if you have a thought, and you simply acknowledge it and do nothing else, you are on your way to having less of an anxious response to that thought.

Take for example the following thoughts. And notice the conversations that can ensue when you engage with your unhelpful thoughts.

Trigger: You see a dent in the lid of the jar of sauce you just purchased

Initial Thought: What if bacteria got into the jar?

Example of Engaging with The Thought: It's just a small dent. It probably didn't break the seal. Maybe I'll open the jar to test out whether the seal is still intact. Okay. There was a small popping sound, but it didn't seem to be as loud as normal. In fact, maybe I just imagined hearing the popping sound. Maybe it didn't make a sound at all. It's definitely possible that the jar was dented, and the seal was broken. If it hasn't been properly sealed, it could be contaminated with Salmonella or Listeria. I could literally die if that's the case. But maybe I should just not worry about it. I've read online that the chances of food contamination in store-bought foods is practically zero. But what if this is one of those unique cases? It would be stupid to assume I'm safe. Wouldn't it? Why take that chance? I'll just throw this jar out and get a new one next time I go shopping. I'll eat something else today. No harm done.

Trigger: You say thank you to someone who just complimented you.

Initial Thought: Was I really genuine when I thanked that person?

Example of Engaging with the Thought: I don't think I really felt thankful enough when I said thank you. It just wasn't genuine. What if I'm just a bad person? I try to smile and be nice to people, but why is it I have to *try* to be nice? Does trying mean I'm not naturally a nice person? I can't tell if I really want to smile at people or not. Sometimes I don't think I really want to smile. I also get annoyed with my one friend a lot. Maybe I really don't like other people. I bet good people don't get annoyed with others like that. And I feel like I have to think about every action I take. I never feel natural. It's like everything I do is fake. I'm just a fake, bad person. Acting like a nice person. I really am the worst.

Instead of engaging with these thoughts, try labeling the initial thought a Worry Thought or a Doubt. Say "thank you" to your brain and then just let the thought hang out as long as it wants. In the meantime, you can direct your attention back to something else far more important in life, like beer brewing, or live action role playing, or extreme couponing.

Don't Try and Erase Your Brain's Messages: We all know how good it can feel to go through our email account, or voicemail, or texting history and delete old messages and free up that memory. Unfortunately, you can't do this with the messages that your brain sends you. Once a thought is in your history, it's there to stay. Part of making peace with your brain is, not only accepting that you don't get to control the messages your brain sends you, but you also don't get to sort through your thought history and clean it up. Once you've had a thought, you're likely to have that thought again at some point in your life. And the more time you've already spent giving that thought your attention, the more likely it is to be an occasional theme in your thoughts, for the immediate future at least. So, keep in mind that there is no way to delete thoughts from your thought history. The solution is actually to become comfortable with these thoughts being a part of your life.

Stay in Control of Your Attention. The zany, disturbing, dark, odd, and gross thoughts your brain comes up with are only one possible target for your attention. Analyzing and questioning your thoughts is a behavior (and, really, a mental ritual) that gives them power and importance. This attention strengthens your thoughts and makes them become more intense themes in your life. Let your Thought Generator do its job in the background and give thoughts your attention when they serve some purpose for you. Thoughts that just make you anxious and worried about things that *might* happen or *might* be true and lead to you getting stuck in your head are typically NOT helpful thoughts. Also, thoughts that can't be proven 100% true or false, or present you with unanswerable questions, or are intrinsically uncertain, are generally not worth your mental activity. When you notice these thoughts grabbing your attention, it's time to disengage from your brain's thought generator and direct your attention elsewhere.

LIVING WITH YOUR
THOUGHT GENERATOR

How to Keep Moving In The Direction You Want To Go

- Realize that your thoughts are not YOU.
- Let your brain be creative and generate random thoughts.
- Be okay with bothersome thoughts, even when they are disturbing possibilities about the future, or the past, or who you are, or what you might be capable of doing.
- Don't try to control your Thought Generator.
- Don't respond mentally or physically to unhelpful thoughts.
- Let your unwanted thoughts play in the background, and focus your attention on other, more helpful, pursuits.

How to End Up On An OCD Exit

- Try to stop your brain from having certain thoughts.
- Try to mentally disprove certain thoughts.
- Ask yourself why your brain just had a thought.
- Try and figure out what your thoughts mean.
- Use repetitive behaviors to try and remove or erase thoughts from your mind.
- Believe that your random thoughts are important.
- Believe that your random thoughts say something about YOU.

Your Memory Drive

In the age of pocket-sized computers, cloud storage and the internet, we are accustomed to retrieving reliable and predictable information whenever we want it. We can pull up the same *Youtube* video over and over again and see the same exact thing every time. And our word processing documents, like the one I'm using to write this book, perfectly preserve all of our edits and changes so that our documents look exactly as it did when we last closed them.

The Memory Drive in your brain could not be more different. As you are experiencing the world, your brain is "recording" things, in a way. But the memories get stored not as hard, concrete, unchanging data files, but as abstract amalgamations of thoughts, images, feelings, hopes and fears, all colored by your own unique perspective on events. With time, they can change, evolve, and even fade completely. The result is an ever-shifting tapestry, part art and part science, that can serve you well in life, as long as you don't push it to be something it's not. Just like a lot of other areas in life, you have to be willing to accept that things are deeply uncertain when it comes to your memory. Our memories are actually quite unreliable, particularly when it comes to the fine details. We routinely forget details from the past as well as add false details to our recollections. And there is actually nothing wrong with you if you can't remember things exactly how they played out. In fact, it is completely normal for people to start statements involving their memories with qualifiers like "I think" or "maybe" or "I'm pretty sure."

Since your recollection of the past is inevitably full of holes, it is a prime area of your life where the OCD doubts and "what if's" can pop up. What if one of those things you can't remember perfectly is a serious threat to your well-being? Once you get pulled into OCD's worries and start looking for absolute answers in your memory banks, you come face to face with all of those gaps and fuzzy areas and question marks in your Memory Drive. And OCD, of course, is more than happy to fill those gaps in your memory with your worst fears. Consider the following back and forth that someone struggling with harm obsessions might have with their doubts:

"Do you remember that night you went out drinking with friends? What if you forced yourself on a woman and don't remember it? Haven't you seen all of those rap victims coming out recently? Maybe you're one of those bad guys."

"Well, I don't remember anything like that happening."

"But you can black out from alcohol. Maybe you just need to search your memory harder."

"I'm trying, but I really don't remember. And I've checked the news every day this week. There have been no unsolved rapes reported."

"Maybe she just hasn't reported it yet."

"But if I don't have any specific memories of anything of the sort happening, and haven't seen anything on the news, that's probably enough reason not to worry."

"Well, it might never get listed in the news. And if you really did this awful thing, this woman might not report it for years. Or, who knows, maybe she just reported it to the police this morning and they are on their way. They might even have video footage of the event."

Once you get sucked into OCD's worries about the past, it never ends, because you never get to pull up the perfect, irrefutable video or data file to silence the doubts. When you try to use your memory to achieve certainty and remove doubt, you are starting down a never-ending road of frustration, anxiety, and dissatisfaction. You are trying to do something with your brain that it cannot do. Let's take a look at how you can better use this amazing function of your brain in a better, more healthy way.

Don't Try and Retrieve Perfect Memories That Are Impervious to Doubts (Especially in The Area of Your Obsessions): In general, your memories can be reliable if you don't push them too hard. They generally provide you with good information about what most likely happened in the past, according to your perspective. So, go ahead and trust them, in general. But once you identify the obsessions related to your OCD diagnosis, you may have to take a different approach with your memories in this area. For example, if you come to realize that you have an OCD obsession that you "might have" done something to hurt yourself or someone else (i.e. you might have poisoned a family member, you might have raped someone and don't remember, you might have overdosed on pills), or that you "might have" forgotten to take an important precaution (locked the doors and windows, turned off your stove or dryer, etc.), you have to realize that you will be highly prone to intrusive doubts about your memory in this area, and that responding to these doubts will never end. You have to resist the urge to search your memory for the certainty you are looking for in this area. You will never connect with a memory that will be impervious to doubts and will inevitably be engaging with your Memory Drive in an inappropriate way. The key is to completely let go of the behavior of reviewing your memory in these areas, and accept the uncertainty of the situation, as painful and anxiety-provoking as that may be.

Set A Limit With OCD: Decide what will be enough evidence for you to worry, and what you can safely file away as "not enough reason to worry." Generally speaking, having a doubt about your memory is not a good reason to worry, particularly when your OCD is sending you non-stop intrusive doubts in a certain area of your life. So, tell OCD "No more! I'm not going to use intrusive doubts about my memory as a reason to obsessively think, worry, and ritualize about something." Now decide what will be a good reason to worry. And here's where you really have to up the stakes on what accounts for good, compelling evidence. Anything short of this leaves OCD too much room to make you worry. Here are some examples of good evidence that you have something to worry about:

- *Checking rituals around leaving appliances on:* I'm not allowed to worry just because I had the thought that I might have left something on. I'm allowed to worry when I get a call from a neighbor or the police or the fire department telling me that my house is on fire.

- *Hit and run OCD:* I'm not allowed to worry just because I had the thought that one of those bumps on the way to work could have been

209

a person. I'm allowed to worry when I can see someone whom I have just hit lying on the street right before my eyes.

- *Harm to self or others:* I'm not allowed to worry that I overdosed just because I have the thought I "may" have taken pills. I am allowed to worry when I'm convulsing on the ground or puking up my guts from an overdose. I'm not allowed to worry that I may have hurt someone because I blacked out while drinking and can't remember everything. I'm allowed to worry when the police are at my door reporting that I did these things.

To further emphasize this strategy of setting a limit with OCD, here are some actual scenarios illustrating this important distinction between intrusive doubts vs. actual evidence of danger:

- *Intrusive Doubt About My Memory:* After passing by the nurse's office in school, it occurred to me that I might have walked into her office and taken a bunch of pills to kill myself. I even think I can taste Tylenol in my mouth.

  Actual Evidence of Danger: I'm on the floor having a seizure and foaming at the mouth because I just ingested a bottle of pills. Signs of my overdose attempt are evident. There are pills strewn all about the floor. The nurse heard me fall to the ground and she is running to my aid.

- *Intrusive Doubt About My Memory:* I think I may want to hurt or kill my family. As we are walking down the sidewalk, I'm pretty sure I just tried to push my Mom into traffic. She doesn't seem fazed, like she didn't even notice it. And I told her I really did try and push her, but she's denying it.

  Actual Evidence of Danger: My Mom is lying on the street screaming because I just pushed her as hard as was absolutely possible to make sure that she fell into the street. A bus is screeching to a stop, but it looks like it is going to run her over.

- *Intrusive Doubt About My Memory:* I think I might have hit someone on the way to work and not remembered it. I'm pretty sure there were a few bumps that were big enough that they could have been a human body or, God forbid, a baby. I could have just zoned out for part of the trip and not noticed it.

Actual Evidence of Danger: I just hit a bump that nearly flipped my car over. Someone on the street is screaming. I pull over. And get out of my car to find a person lying bloody on the road behind my car. A pedestrian is pointing at me and talking on their phone, probably speaking to 911.

- *Intrusive Doubt About My Memory:* I think I might have forgotten to turn off the stove. And I think I might have checked before leaving the house but I'm not totally sure. And I think I might have already returned home once to check again, but I can't be sure of that either. I might just be making that up. I feel like my house is going to burn to the ground if I don't check again.

Actual Evidence of Danger: I just received a call from the fire department while at work. My house is in flames and they are trying to put out the fire.

As extreme as these measures may seem, this is exactly what you have to do with your OCD in this area. You have to set a clear line in the sand, and resist responding to doubts around your memory drive. Over the years, your travel buddy, OCD, has convinced you to assume that you might be in danger, and to never become too comfortable. You're going to have to try the opposite here: assume that you're safe until you encounter irrefutable evidence that something bad has happened. The more you practice getting into this state of mind, the easier it will become. And don't forget the alternative; staying stuck because you're trying to achieve the impossible with your Memory Drive.

211

MANAGING YOUR
MEMORY DRIVE

How to Keep Moving In The Direction You Want To Go

- Accept that you will never be able to use your memory to achieve 100% certainty about the past.
- Choose to resist searching your memory for answers, particularly in the area of your obsessions.
- Allow your brain to generate intrusive thoughts and doubts about the past. Let these play in the background of your life just like any other unhelpful thoughts.
- Require more evidence that you are in danger than just having thoughts, doubts, or "possible" memories in your head.
- Don't worry about things that "might" have happened in the past, unless there is immediate, compelling evidence right before your eyes.
- Don't use checking rituals to remove intrusive doubts from your mind.

How to End Up On An OCD Exit

- Try to retrieve perfect, irrefutable memories.
- Give attention to intrusive doubts about your memories.
- Try to mentally fill in gaps in your memory from times when you may have zoned out (while driving) or blacked out (from a night of drinking).
- Give attention to thoughts about what "might" have happened in the past that don't also include evidence right in front of you in the present.
- Try to use your memory to achieve certainty and remove doubt.

Your Virtual Reality Theater

Another incredible function of your brain is its ability to conjure up full sensory experiences in your imagination that transport you from the reality of your immediate environment. You can tap into this personal Virtual Reality Theater right this very moment. All you have to do is think of one of your favorite people, a favorite food, a song you like, or your favorite season, and notice the sensory experience that ensues. You will undoubtedly "see" that person, "taste" your favorite food, "hear" your favorite song, and "smell" your favorite season, even though these things are not present in your environment. The Virtual Reality Theater is one of the reasons why life as a human being is so rich, full, and amazing, but it can cause us a lot of difficulty as well. In addition to giving you access to the sensory experiences you enjoy, your brain can conjure up experiences you don't like as well – giving you feelings of nausea that convince you that you are sick, or giving you a disgusted feeling that makes you believe you are "dirty," or causing you to feel anxiety that makes it hard to ignore the possibility you might have cancer. Consider the following examples of the Virtual Reality Theater causing major difficulties in the lives of several people with OCD:

Sunita is struggling with a fear of developing a shellfish allergy and going into anaphylactic shock. She has never experienced an actual episode and has tested negative for shellfish allergies. However, she is bothered by intrusive thoughts that she could develop an allergy at any point in her life. Her fears can become triggered whenever she is near seafood, even to the point of just walking by a restaurant that serves seafood. Once her fear and anxiety set in, she will experience a sensation of her throat tightening, an uneasy feeling in her stomach, and dizziness. Since she does not have a seafood allergy, these symptoms are identified as somatic symptoms caused by her anxiety. Whenever she has the symptoms, however, she chooses to explore them and ask herself what they could be. This takes her further into her imagination where she becomes fully convinced that she is having an anaphylactic episode.

Alex is struggling with an irrational fear that he will turn into another person. Specifically, he fears that he will turn into one of the mean kids in his school, through either contamination from their germs or thinking about them. Sometimes at night, Alex will accidentally think of one of the mean kids in school and become fearful that he is changing into one of them. He will actually "feel" his face changing, and when he looks in the mirror, he can "see" changes in his appearance. These experiences sometimes convince him to the point of inducing panic attacks. He is frustrated to be struggling with a fear that is so irrational, but he can't help repeatedly being convinced by the full sensory experiences that his brain's Virtual Reality Theater creates.

Briana is experiencing intense fears that others are talking about her. Whenever interacting with her coworkers, she struggles to battle the thoughts and images of her colleagues talking and laughing about her when she's not around. Briana will often have vivid images of her coworkers, who are always pleasant and cordial with her in person, being completely different behind her back. She will see scenes of them laughing and talking about her with disdain. Her OCD keeps reminding her that it is possible for people to be completely different when she's not around. And these disturbing sensory experiences full of images and sounds have actually impacted the way she sees her coworkers, causing her to doubt their words and behavior in her presence. The reality is that none of these incidents of coworkers discussing her, criticizing her, or laughing at her have occurred in the slightest. And yet, the Virtual Reality Theater of her mind has done quite the job of cementing these imaginary scenes in her mind.

Let's look at some strategies you can use to manage your Virtual Reality Theater when you are having convincing OCD sensory experiences.

When in Doubt, Seek Out Professional Advice (to Start): If you are worried that you might be losing your eyesight, or that your house is contaminated with lead paint, or that you could have a heart condition, or any other serious concern, make sure that you seek out the appropriate and necessary care. Talk to your doctor. Have your house tested for lead paint. And take the appropriate precautions recommended by that professional. And when you're really struggling to decide if something is a real concern or an OCD obsession, seek out the guidance of a mental health professional adequately trained to treat OCD. Once you've taken the recommended precautions, and identified your ongoing concern as an OCD obsession, you are ready to face the virtual reality experience of your OCD.

Time to Stop "Figuring Out" If Your Fears Are Coming True: Difficulties with the Virtual Reality Theater arise when you are committed to "figuring out" if your fears are happening each time you experience a new OCD episode. Engaging in this thought process will inevitably lead you to become absorbed in your imagination, where thoughts will trigger anxiety and physical sensations, as well as cause you to imagine other sensory experiences. Once you've entered into the imagination, it becomes very hard to disengage from the experience. Better to not even put yourself in that position by stopping yourself from trying to answer the "what if's" and doubts that lead there. You can then keep your attention on the world outside of your mind and body. As you notice worry thoughts, and accompanying feelings and sensations, acknowledge them but don't attempt to review and/or process them. You can even say to yourself, there's the "worry trick" or the "virtual reality experience" again. Then choose to return your attention to a more productive use of your time. You will find that removing the "figuring it out" ritual can actually help to reduce some of your distress from the situation, and also prevent you from getting pulled into your imagination.

Make Sure You Are Completing Planned Exposures: Being triggered in the moment by convincing virtual reality experiences is extremely difficult to challenge. It's important that you complete planned exposures on a daily basis to challenge your fears at a time when you feel in control of the experience. The benefit of this is that you will have already faced your fears purposefully by the time you are triggered randomly out there in the wild. Those repeated planned exposures will pay off when those natural exposures are a little bit less triggering and a little easier to challenge. So, go out and write exposure scripts, watch triggering videos, write triggering stories, do those things that make you have to experience anxiety symptoms in a safe, controlled environment. If you're afraid of panic attacks, make yourself dizzy or do something to increase your heart rate. If you're afraid of throwing up, spin in an office chair, drink water until you're full, or do other things that make you have sensations in your stomach. If you're afraid you're going to snap and become violent, allow yourself to be angry with someone and even tell them that you're angry. If you fear you'll lose your eyesight, stare at a wall and notice all the strange things in your vision on purpose. If you can regularly move in the direction of what makes you nervous, you will find that those triggering moments become a little bit more manageable.

What You Choose to Focus on Has an Impact. Watching a horror movie is going to put you in a completely different mental space than watching a comedy. And the same holds true for what mental experiences you choose to give your attention. When you choose to focus on the possibility you could be soon dying of cancer and end up imagining the scene of your funeral, that is going to have a huge impact on you. The same can be said for immersively imagining yourself going to hell or losing your sanity or being the laughingstock of everyone you know or ending up homeless on the streets. Identify the repetitive experiences your imagination is conjuring up for you and notice how you feel when you explore them. You may discover that this habit of focusing on certain thought content is having a negative impact on your emotions, your mood, and your outlook. When you notice that you end up feeling awful every time you focus on specific mental content, realize that you have the choice to direct your attention towards other things. Start to catch yourself "watching the show" and practice gently disengaging from the experience. Then let the Virtual Reality Theater fade into the background and choose to direct your attention elsewhere. It won't stop the thoughts and the feelings, but you will stop accepting your brain's invitation to enter into your imagination and .

LIVING WITH YOUR

VIRTUAL REALITY THEATER

How to Keep Moving In The Direction You Want To Go

- Realize that OCD can manufacture extremely convincing, "real-feeling" experiences.
- Don't explore intrusive doubts and "what if's," and allow them to pull you into your imagination.
- Reduce thinking behaviors such as rumination that pull you away from the world of your senses.
- Tolerate the physical symptoms of anxiety without trying to "figure out" what they mean.
- Focus your attention on experiences in the world of your senses when thoughts are trying to pull you into your imagination.
- Trust the experience of your senses in the real world more than the "OCD story" that unfolds in your head.

How to End Up On An OCD Exit

- Follow intrusive doubts and "what if's" into your imagination whenever they are triggered.
- Try to figure out if your OCD experience is real danger each and every time you are triggered.
- Try and figure out what the feelings and sensations mean whenever you are triggered.
- Do not identify other real-world targets for your attention when you are triggered.
- Allow yourself to repeatedly enter into your imagination where the "OCD story" feels true.

217

Your Alarm System

Another of your brain's major functions is the regulation of your emotions. In the most basic terms, emotions are nothing more than immersive physical sensations triggered by your brain that are supposed to alert you to events in your surroundings and motivate you to behave in a particular manner. You might call them your internal Alarm System. In the same way that having a hungry feeling is supposed to alert you to the fact that you haven't eaten (and compel you to seek out food), the tense physical sensation of anger is meant to warn you that something unfair is going on (and trigger you to become more aggressive), the painful feeling of guilt is supposed to alert you that you've done something wrong (and motivate you to seek repentance), and the complex sensations of anxiety warn you of danger (and ready you to face a threat by either fighting or making a quick getaway). Your Alarm System is meant to be a shortcut. It helps you to circumvent the time-consuming process of "thinking" and "deciding what to do" and cuts right to an automatic behavioral response. As an example, if you happen to cross the street without looking both ways, and see a truck rumbling straight towards you, the last thing you want to do is waste time "deciding" if you should move out of the way or not. And thanks to anxiety, you don't have to. Thanks to your trusty Alarm System, your brain notices the threat, triggers the physical sensations of anxiety, and you are compelled to leap out of the way. No thinking necessary.

Sort of like your Thought Generator, the Alarm System of your brain is always running in the background and does its thing without any input from you. It also comes with some pre-programming at birth. Specific triggers are supposed to lead to specific emotions, each of which correspond to specific behavioral responses. Most of us, for example, have similar general triggers. A majority of people experience fear in response to snakes and spiders. We are all disgusted by human waste. And most of us become upset when we see someone dangerously ignoring traffic laws. But we each have our own quirks too, with our individual emotions having a unique set of triggers. Some of us get annoyed by people chewing while others don't seem to notice. Some of us are filled with joy in summer. Others just want to get in from the heat.

And we all have strong, unique preferences in almost all areas of life, most of which are dictated by the emotions that things make us feel. No matter the individual quirks, thought, we all want our Alarm Systems to be helpful to us. When the Alarm System is working as it should, we should feel guilty when we've actually done something wrong, we should feel disgusted when something is confirmed visibly to be "contaminated," and we should feel anxious when we are faced with some sort of important, looming threat. OCD, however, can wreak havoc on one's Alarm System. OCD can cause your Alarm System to trigger emotions at the "wrong" time and cause you to become stuck behaving in ways that are maladaptive to your situation. You suddenly feel like you need to clean, or repent, or avoid, or escape when there isn't a good reason for doing so. Here is a more in depth look at some of the common emotions associated with OCD:

Anger: Anger is an emotion that generally occurs in response to unfairness. When something is happening that feels unjust, or is hurtful to you in some way, your brain triggers the anger emotion in an effort to get you to do something about the injustice. Anger can trigger the following internal experiences and impulses: 1) looking out for yourself, 2) believing you are completely in the right 3) believing everyone else is wrong, and 4) increased motivation to right the wrong immediately, by force if necessary. In situations where something extremely unfair is happening to you, you can see how this would be a very helpful mental shortcut. And if you think of past time periods when there may have been less societal protection in place such as law enforcement and the courts, you can imagine how the individual would have had to right wrongs on their own. (i.e., you would have had to club the caveman or cavewoman who just took your piece of meat in order to get it back and make sure it didn't happen again). In situations where you are getting the anger emotion at the wrong time, however, you can also see how it can become extremely unhelpful to be in this mindset.

Guilt: Human beings are social animals. And we have always needed one another in order to survive, particularly in the harsh conditions of humanity's past when we were surrounded by bigger, more vicious creatures. The last thing you would have wanted was to be left out in the wild on your own. The emotion of guilt is one way that we would have kept our own behavior in check and remained on good terms with our group. Throw in religion, and you can start to feel guilty whenever you fear you may have disappointed or hurt your standing with God. When you've done something insensitive, mean, or hurtful to a friend or family member, to God, or even to society, your brain triggers the guilty feeling in an effort to get you to correct your standing. Some of the things that come with the guilty feeling include: 1) intense humility 2) a desire to put your own needs aside in exchange for the person you have wronged, and 3) a desire to experience punishment. Again, you can see how adaptive this human emotion has been for human societies, past and present. But, then again, you can see how unhelpful and incapacitating it would be to have this emotion occurring at the wrong time.

Disgust: Disgust is another extremely powerful emotion. From a survival standpoint, it is meant to protect us from unsafe circumstances. It is no coincidence that we are 'disgusted' by feces and spoiled or rotten food, as well as filth and dirt in general. These are potential health hazards to us if consumed. Some of the behaviors associated with feeling disgusted involve: 1) Getting away from or avoiding the "contaminated" object or area, 2) cleaning yourself and your environment and 3) preserving any clean or uncontaminated areas. Again, this emotion is extremely powerful and uncomfortable and can be severely impairing when it is being triggered by everyday situations such as walking into a public restroom, touching a door, or being near another person, which often occurs in OCD.

Anxiety: When you are anxious, you are supposed to feel like you have to stop something and do whatever it takes. You are supposed to believe that the presence of anxiety means something important or dangerous is happening, and that you should, under no circumstances, stop worrying and relax until the anxiety is gone. You're supposed to trust your anxiety. And our anxiety emotion is actually quite good at convincing us that this is the case. Consequently, the time between having an anxious response and completing an anxious behavior is often non-existent. That is how good our anxiety is at controlling us. In many cases, this is extremely helpful. If you feel a very concerning sensation in your internal body, you should be making a doctor's appointment instead of playing video games. People with OCD, however, will often develop an overly active anxious response in the area of their obsession. Because your fear of a specific consequence is so strong, anything that even remotely reminds you of that fear will cause anxiety.

Joy: It is important to recognize that there are also positive emotions that are meant to reinforce our behavior as well. When we are around the people and places that "complete" us, when we do something selfless for others, when we are successful at something, our brain can also cause us to feel the joy feeling. Some of the things associated with joy include 1) a desire to repeat the behavior and/or experience causing the joy, 2) a desire to be near the people causing the joy. The important thing to know about joy, with regards to OCD, is that you can get so wrapped up in avoiding your triggers and getting rid of your negative emotions, that you forget to notice the things that bring you joy and to plan to incorporate those things into your life more.

When you have OCD, the thoughts associated with your obsessions trigger certain emotions. Contamination thoughts tend to trigger disgust. Fears of being a bad person or immoral in some way tend to trigger guilt. And health-related fears tend to trigger anxiety. And since your OCD thoughts and fears are exaggerated and/or irrational responses to everyday life, you end up stuck with emotions at the wrong time. You are stuck with a level of anxiety appropriate for encountering a bear in the woods when you are simply studying for a quiz. Or you feel the guilt equivalent to having just killed someone when you neglect to pick up a piece of litter. Or you experience the disgust akin to stepping into a port-a-potty that hasn't been cleaned in a week, when you touch a doorknob in your house. Your Alarm System is basically encountering some problems.

But here's a little-known secret; your Alarm System is actually reprogrammable. You have to set some realistic expectations in this department, of course. Don't forget that your Alarm System is another function of your flawed human brain, and not an app on your tablet. Reprogramming it can be a slow and difficult process, but totally worth it. You can actually weaken or strengthen the emotions your Alarm System is generating in response to triggers. If you experience anxiety or guilt or anger in response to something in life, and you respond to this emotion by trying to avoid your triggers, or ritualize in some way, you will strengthen that emotional response. The more you avoid the trigger, the stronger and stronger the emotional response will become when you are forced to encounter that trigger. So, if you get a disgusted response one day in a public restroom and decide to start avoiding them, that disgust response will be strengthened every time you avoid a public restroom. But here's the really great news. The opposite is also true. If you start to go to public restrooms again, the strength of that disgust emotion will gradually weaken. The first visit will be the worst, and it may not get better the 2nd, 3rd, or 4th time. But if you stick with it, the Alarm System will eventually tire of sending out such a strong signal. Week to week, month to month, you will reprogram your Alarm System.

Accept Your Emotions: While your Alarm System *is* reprogrammable, this is a process. It can take weeks, months, and even years to engage in enough exposure to reprogram your emotions. This means that, in the meantime, you have to stop wishing for your emotions to stop. When, and if your Alarm System decides to trigger an emotion, and how long that emotion will last is largely outside of our control. In other words, you don't get to decide what emotion you are feeling at every given moment. As you work to challenge your OCD, be sure to take that first step and accept the existence of the emotions you don't like. They're happening. And they are going to continue to happen for some time. It's also important to realize that as you take the proper steps to treat your OCD, and start to do things you've been avoiding doing, you will most likely start to feel these emotions more often, and at a greater intensity, than you've been feeling them up to now.

Pay Attention to Your Body: OCD can cause you to become overly fixated on their mind and its thoughts. You might view your OCD struggle as a purely cognitive battle with your thoughts and become overly focused on a thinking solution to your problems. This can cause you to completely overlook a huge part of the problem; the emotions that you feel when you are experiencing the thoughts. So, what is the problem with this? Well, if you are not paying attention to your emotions, you are not going to be ready for what you have to tolerate to beat your OCD. You are going to be giving into OCD over and over again because an emotion that you are not aware of is making you avoid and do your rituals. To start working on this, it is important that you notice exactly what your emotions feel like. The next time you are triggered, see if you can identify where that guilt, or anger, or anxiety shows up in your body. Is there a tightness in your muscles? A tension in your neck and back? Does it feel like your stomach is "sinking?" Or your chest is tightening? Or your heart is pounding? Do you get a headache? Notice whatever it is that you are feeling. And then relax your muscles and accept those physical sensations. Notice how "bad" the feeling actually is? See how long you are able to tolerate it? You may actually find that when you focus on how it actually feels to have a certain emotion, that it is not as bad as you have been thinking it is. Once you have identified the specific sensations you experience with your triggered emotion, that sets the stage for your new goals. You are going to have to get good at feeling bad. As part of your exposure process, notice the emotions that get triggered, and work on increasing the amount of time you can tolerate those physical sensations without ritualizing and/or escaping.

Don't Pay Too Much Attention to Your Emotions: On the flipside, you can actually develop a fixation on your emotions. Do you find yourself constantly "checking in" with your emotions to see how anxious you are? When someone asks you how things are going, do you immediately jump into a status update on your current emotional state? This may indicate that you are prioritizing your emotions over other important things in life. This can lead to excessive "waiting" to start something if you don't feel like your emotions are in the right place. If you are struggling with this sort of approach to life, work to shift your relationship with your emotions. Instead of checking in with your emotions to decide what you are going to do in a particular moment, use other criteria to guide your behavior. Try making decisions based on what you WANT or NEED to do, rather than how you are feeling. Practice ignoring the signals from your Alarm System and continuing to move towards your goals.

LIVING WITH YOUR
ALARM SYSTEM

How to Keep Moving In The Direction You Want To Go

- Realize that feelings are not facts.
- Accept that you can't control your emotions.
- Get to know the physical sensations that characterize your emotions.
- Get used to feeling the emotions you don't like.
- Welcome all feelings into your life. They are there whether you want them to be or not.
- Let your emotions come and go like the weather.
- Realize that OCD is making you feel certain feelings at the wrong time. They are not trustworthy signals.

How to End Up On An OCD Exit

- Try to control what emotions you are feeling.
- Use rituals to try and remove emotions you don't like.
- Believe that your feelings are trustworthy and legitimate every time your OCD makes you anxious, guilty, disgusted, etc.
- Believe that feelings are facts.
- Keep resisting your emotions.
- Don't familiarize yourself with your emotions by noticing the sensations they bring.

Your Problem Solver

Your brain's ability to solve problems is amazing. You can use the Problem Solver function of your brain to analyze the various parts of a problem, identify potential solutions, and put a plan into action. You can use it to figure out a childcare solution on a snow day, figure out how to manage a semester of 20 credits, and plan and successfully carry out your Florida vacation. It's also the part of our brains that has allowed us, as a species, to cure diseases and send a rover to Mars.

But the amazingness of your Problem Solver can lead you to overuse this function of your brain. You can start to see everything in life as a "problem" needing to be fixed, and your Problem Solver as the solution. And when you use the Problem Solver in situations when it's not helpful, that's when you get stuck, trying and trying to fix problems that refuse to be solved. Many of the things that you "don't like" in life are not things you can ever change. The answer isn't to "solve" them. The answer is to accept and tolerate them. With this in mind, let's look at some guidelines for effectively using your Problem Solver:

Identify What Constitutes a Problem That You Can Solve: The following are appropriate problems to address with your brain's Problem Solver. With all of these tasks, you can identify a clear, solvable problem, brainstorm possible solutions, and take clear steps to implement a satisfactory fix to the problem.

- *You have to figure out what size curtains to buy.* You find yourself a tape measure. You measure your windows. You write down those measurements and bring them to the store. And you purchase yourself a beautiful set of perfectly sized curtains in neutral tones.

- *You have to complete a math problem.* You review the problem and identify the appropriate application you have to use. You follow the steps in the required sequence and arrive at the correct answer.

- *You have to plan a family vacation.* You identify your destination. You purchase your hotel accommodations. You purchase your round-trip

225

airfare. You request your vacation days and wait for your plans to all come together. Or you just hire a travel agent and have someone do it all for you. Either way, a solution is achievable.

- *You have to figure out a childcare solution on a snow day.* You call your parents, only to find out your Dad has an eye appointment. You contact any and all people in the neighborhood you think might be staying home with their kids. On your fifth try, Gina down the street is happy to take the little tikes for the day. You drop them off, thank Gina profusely, and finally drive to work, wondering why they cancelled school with just an inch of snow.

The following examples, on the other hand, rather than being problems, are inevitable realities in life. Any attempt to try and solve these "problems" will only lead to frustration, since none of these life circumstances can actually be solved.

- *You don't complete a task perfectly.* To be imperfect is to be human. If you think of imperfection" as a problem needing to be solved, you're going to have a really hard time navigating a typical day and completing rudimentary tasks of life.

- *You don't like your physical appearance.* Sure, you can make small improvements to your appearance. You can work out. Get a haircut. But for the most part, this is the body you're stuck with. Unless you're rich and can afford to make not-so-great life decisions with a plastic surgeon, you don't get to order a different body. So be careful not to use that Problem Solver and convince yourself that you're somehow going to find a way to slip into a new body. Might as well get used to the one you've got.

- *You don't know which choice will result in the best future outcome.* Until someone invents a time machine, you're going to have to accept the inevitable uncertainty in the future. You don't get to completely find out the results of your choices until you actually make them.

- *You feel anxious.* Life causes anxiety.

- *You're having a thought you don't like.* Your brain is a creative, thought generating machine with no filter. And it thinks what it wants to think.

- *You're feeling a feeling you don't like.* On a moment-to-moment basis, your Alarm System is largely out of your control, so try and resist that urge to control your emotions. And once you start to use exposure to reduce an unhelpful emotional response you've been having, don't forget that this process takes time and, ironically, you have to purposefully expose yourself to the emotions you don't like, to reduce their frequency.

- *You're upset by how you performed socially.* You've messed up before and you're bound to mess up again, no matter how many times you review your performance in your head. And that's okay.

If you find yourself trying to solve "problems" like these that can't actually be solved, try the following strategy for breaking this habit:

Control When You Use Your Problem Solver: The Problem Solver is one of those functions of your brain that you actually have a fair amount of control over. You get to decide if the issue you're facing is an actual solvable problem, or simply something in life that you don't like but can't change. For things in the latter category, take care not to engage in any of the following thinking behaviors in response:

- Trying to "figure things out" all of the time
- Reviewing past situations over and over in your head
- Trying to predict what will happen in the future
- Trying to change things about the world that are outside of your control
- Over-thinking
- Constantly analyzing
- Being overly critical

EFFECTIVELY USING YOUR
PROBLEM SOLVER

How to Keep Moving In The Direction You Want To Go

- Accept the uncertainty in your life.
- Accept the reality of risk in your life.
- Make imperfect decisions.
- Accept that you have to move forward and live in order to see the outcomes of your decisions.
- Accept that you can't predict the future.
- Accept that "not liking" something does not mean it's a problem to be eradicated.
- Accept that things don't always need to be understood and "figured out."

How to End Up On An OCD Exit

- Try to "solve" things that are not problems but inescapable realities in your life.
- Try to make perfect, guaranteed decisions.
- Try to remove uncertainty from your life.
- Try to remove risk from your life.
- Try to "figure things out" all the time.
- Try to change things over and over again that don't ever seem to change.
- Constantly analyze everything.
- Try and "fix" everything in life you don't like.

Chapter 7

Time to Get Rid of Some of Your Baggage (aka Let Go of the Past)

This book is all about creating a new start in life. It's about going on a trip to rediscover your true self and change the relationship you have with your OCD. As you continue on this journey, you're going to want to travel light. The less baggage the better. But you should also know that the longer you've had OCD, the more baggage you may have amassed over the years. Bad memories. Weakened relationships. Regrets. Lost confidence. Distorted thoughts about yourself as someone who's weird or "different" or weak. OCD can cause some damage sometimes. You may be trying your best not to think about these things, hoping you can let the past be the past, but noticing that the past won't leave you alone. Your baggage, just as much as your current OCD symptoms, can sometimes prevent you from being the person you want to be. So this final chapter exists to help you root out any of those OCD demons that may still be keeping you stuck. It might be time to start to think differently about any of the bad stuff OCD may have caused in your life, and let those bad feelings go.

There's no other way to put it. OCD can make you do some really weird things. When you have OCD, it is practically a given that you've acted in ways you're embarrassed about. You may not be proud of how you've treated others. Or you may be feeling bad about what you've done (or not done) with your time. Let me share a few stories from people I've met through my private practice that demonstrate some of the embarrassing predicaments I've seen OCD create:

Jack: Around the time when Jack hit puberty, he, like all young men, started to masturbate on occasion. At the same time, because of his OCD, he developed a fear that he might get his Mom pregnant by contaminating objects in the house with his semen. In order to avoid this feared scenario, Jack developed painstaking rituals; a lengthy shower ritual, a clearing regimen for his bathroom, and a strict schedule for changing his sheets. In the summer, he would often just jump into the backyard pool, fully clothed, to decontaminate himself. Unfortunately, despite his best efforts to carefully prevent the spread of the contamination, due to various "mistakes" when a handwash was missed or contaminated item was not properly handled, Jack ended up contaminating numerous areas of his bedroom. The room became off limits to all others in the family. When I first met Jack, he had yet to tell another living soul about why he was engaging in these compulsive behaviors. His embarrassment and shame were that deep.

Amy: Amy rubbed shoulders with her younger brother one afternoon while she was home from college and noticed a sensation in her pubic area that she could only assume to be sexual arousal. She began to fear that she was incestuous and a pedophile. In her words, she feared that she was "a monster." When she returned to college, she began to avoid phone contact with her brother for fear of experiencing more feelings of attraction. She eventually learned that her brother experienced a difficult quarter in high school and fought constantly with their parents during this period when she did not talk to him. On top of feeling like "a monster," Amy also developed feelings of intense guilt for not having been there for her brother.

Evan: Evan developed a fear that he might "catch" autism as if it were an airborne illness. He soon found it difficult to attend school because of the numerous autistic peers with whom he shared the hallways and classrooms. Evan began waiting until everyone else had left the hallway before walking to class, which caused him to repeatedly get into trouble. He developed extensive washing and showering rituals at home. He was unable to bring anything home that had come into contact with the school, including his textbooks and clothes. He also began engaging in "breathing rituals" that involved slowly breathing in through his nose and breathing out through the side of his mouth. He would be unable to speak until completing this breath, so when people asked him questions there would be a long delay before he responded. This made him fear that he appeared "slow," which only worsened his OCD fears that he might be catching autism.

Reading through these examples, if you're like most people, you're probably thinking "Man. OCD can be rough" or "I really feel for these folks" (a natural, empathic reaction). But for the individuals mentioned above, they spent years thinking that people would think they were crazy or weird if anyone ever found out. That's the plight of OCD. It makes you do all sorts of crazy things that you don't really want to be doing and then, as a cherry on top, makes you feel really guilty and ashamed about those behaviors.

So, we have to do something about this situation. I can assure you that the people above are all the coolest, most "typical" people you could ever meet, and they are walking around with all of this undeserved guilt. And it's not just them. All around the world, people with OCD are feeling guilty and ashamed. And you probably are too. Let's see what we can do to start to address this epidemic.

So Much to Be Embarrassed About. Or Is There?

First, like with so many things with OCD, we have to put all the cards on the table. No secrets. No avoidance. Secrecy and avoidance are like pure diesel fuel for OCD. They give OCD its power. So, let's start off with a list of all the goofy, awkward, embarrassing things that OCD may have caused you to do, and that you may be holding onto. Let's review the baggage, shall we?

Shame Baggage: OCD has a way of making you feel like you're not worthy of doing anything in life. It can convince you that it doesn't really matter whether or not you have things like friends or goals. It doesn't want you to stand up for yourself and say "I'm worth it. I deserve to follow my desired path through life." That's why it's so important to challenge OCD's assumptions about you. Remember. You are human. You are not better or worse than any other human being out there. And yes, you make mistakes. And yes, you have done bad or "wrong" things. This doesn't mean that there is something wrong with you or that you need to resign yourself to a lifetime of ritualizing. Let yourself say it. "I'm worthy." "I'm good enough."

231

Weird Baggage: You've probably engaged in unusual OCD rituals, like twisting the cap on and off your water bottle five times every time you want to drink from it, breathing in a strange manner, doing a crazy routine of scrubbing and pumping soap and drying your hands a very specific way every time you wash your hands, getting stuck in your head and spacing out while others are trying to talk to you, having red, inflamed skin on your face from picking at blemishes in the mirror. Some of these things have probably been witnessed by others even though you've tried your best to hide them.

Frustration Baggage: Frustration can occur when your OCD symptoms cause you to do things you don't want to be doing. For example, you might know deep down that your OCD fears of eating the last bite of food or talking to girls are ridiculous. And so, you may experience chronic frustration that you are stuck with a fear that you don't even agree with. And yet, this frustration and, relatedly, this lack of acceptance of your OCD symptoms, can hold you back from effectively managing your OCD. You may be so consumed with frustration that you're making things even harder on yourself because instead of just having a fear, now you have a fear and frustration to deal with whenever you are triggered. It might be time to take that step and accept the existence of your OCD symptoms, including the irrational thoughts, intense emotions, and the out-of-the-ordinary behaviors. Even when you've got the OCD under control, these symptoms will occasionally pop up. And that's okay.

Controlling Baggage: As someone struggling with OCD, you may have acted in a controlling way by telling others in your life to act and speak a certain way and using anger and other strategies to get them to comply: making your wife reassure you endlessly about your relationship, making your Mom say the same prayer over and over again at night until she says it just right, demanding that everyone else in the house keep things clean and uncontaminated. Feeling like a "controlling" person isn't all that great. But just know that you've been struggling, and you've been hurting, and that changing this behavior is possible, one step at a time.

Mean Baggage: You may have developed some uncharacteristic mean behaviors like lashing out at others when your OCD is triggered, making really biting insults that you don't really mean, yelling at others for not "doing it right" when they are trying to get you through an OCD episode, breaking and smashing things, even hitting others when you've gone into a rage. These are all very typical OCD behaviors. The important thing is that, once you're aware of them, you owe it to yourself and others to work on these behaviors and gradually reduce them. And, as far as those times when you weren't at your best, don't forget that you're struggling with a real, genuine mental health issue called OCD and you're allowed to forgive yourself for those moments.

Emotional Baggage: When your emotions have run high, you've lost the ability to control your behavior and have had some extreme meltdowns/tantrums. Maybe you've gone on intense OCD rants when triggered or shared all of your irrational OCD thoughts and fears out loud when triggered. Having shown your emotions in this way is what has allowed you to see how bad your OCD has gotten. And it has allowed others a window into your world so that they can see just how difficult life with OCD has been for you.

Neglectful Baggage: Having OCD has possibly led you to turn down invitations from friends, miss holiday dinners with family, fail classes, lose jobs, and sabotage romantic relationships. As important as these things are in life, you've had to focus attention on OCD. You've had to experience it worsening, identify it, understand it, find your motivation, and start to work on it. These things take incredible amounts of time and motivation. And it's incredibly sad to miss opportunities, but you're not alone in this regard. Everyone has regrets. Allow yourself to mourn those things but realize that amazing things can happen at any point in your life and they don't all have to happen according to the rest of the world's schedule.

Time Wasting Baggage: Your OCD may have led you to lose large amounts of time by making you spend 2 hours getting ready in the morning due to OCD rituals, check your desk 20 times before leaving the office, turn

233

back and make sure you didn't hit anyone on your drive to work, spend hours online researching about your obsession. Making peace with this lost time is going to require you to set different standards for yourself. Remember that you are someone living with OCD who has so much to be proud of just being where you are right now. Seek out people in your life that understand the struggles that have taken up that time and who are proud of you. Identify the successes you've had. Find the pride you have for yourself. And don't forget that it's never too late to find time in the present to set new goals for yourself.

Guilty Baggage: When you feel like you have made life miserable and difficult for those around you, you can get saddled with a chronic guilty feeling. Thinking that you have been a burden, that you have worsened the physical health of those around you, and/or have caused a financial burden on them; these are all very common parts of the struggle with OCD. This is an area where it is extremely important that you learn to separate yourself from your OCD. When you are too fused with your OCD, it's all too easy to say "I" caused these things. But that is forgetting that you have been diagnosed with a mental health issue. And, just like any other medical issue in life, it causes difficulties for the sufferer and the people around them, and it requires time and money to engage in the treatment. Remember that you never asked to have OCD and those around you who really love you would do anything, and should do anything, to help you with your mental health diagnosis.

Family Baggage: This one's about the baggage that may not be coming from you but from others. For many younger people living with OCD, you may have had to hear from your parents and others that you aren't working on things, and aren't working hard enough. This can be discouraging and make you want to throw in the towel. Perhaps, more importantly it can strain your relationships with those people. You might feel misunderstood and unsupported. In this case, it's hard to say whether those individuals will ever come around and notice the work you've done and the changes you've made. Only you can make this decision, but give some consideration to forgiving those in your life who have lacked patience and understanding, and who have not been able to deal with this whole OCD situation. If this baggage is really holding you down, forgiveness may be the key to you being able to travel a little bit lighter.

Don't Feel Bad About the Symptoms of Your OCD

It's time to do something about this extra baggage you've been lugging around. Think about some of the other conditions people are regularly struggling with. And ask yourself if you think someone with asthma should feel embarrassed that they have to use an inhaler when they become short of breath? Do you believe that someone born with imperfect vision should recoil in humiliation when they're unable to read a sign without their glasses on? Of course not. And you probably know the next question. Why should you feel embarrassed for experiencing all of the symptoms of having OCD? Let's review some of the symptoms of OCD that occur with almost anyone who has it:

- Engaging in repetitive rituals that may seem unusual to others who aren't familiar with OCD

- Losing focus and attention, and spacing out, when getting stuck in your obsessive thoughts

- Making decisions based on what will lower your anxiety and get rid of intrusive thoughts rather than what are the best, most helpful, most socially aware, and most practical decisions

- Focusing a lot of attention on managing your own internal mental health struggles, to the point that you haven't been a support for others in your life

- Requiring breaks from school and work to address your mental health needs and engage in required treatments

- Having to adjust goals, and the timelines for those goals, to account for the existence of a serious mental health issue.

- Experiencing relationship conflict when you don't have your symptoms properly managed

235

- Feeling isolated because you haven't been able to share the details of your struggle with others and haven't found anyone who can relate to what you're going through

These are all pretty standard symptoms of OCD, and unfortunately also happen to be some things that people with OCD can feel pretty bad about. But if OCD didn't cause problems for people, there probably wouldn't even be a need for a diagnosis called OCD.

Blame the OCD, Not Yourself

That list of OCD symptoms above, just like the difficulty breathing that comes with asthma, and the impaired vision that comes with being near-sighted, are part of the OCD diagnosis. Work on accepting these phenomena as symptoms of OCD rather than strikes against your personality, or your motivation, or your character. Once you can identify the difficulties and embarrassing moments and painful events you've experienced as OCD symptoms, you now have an appropriate target for your blame. Your OCD is the reason for those times when you've done something embarrassing, or weren't there for family and friends, or weren't strong enough, or lost your cool, or made a poor decision.

Now the complementary situation that comes with blaming OCD is, of course, taking that blame off of yourself. Finally. You've been anxious, controlled by emotions, not knowing which thoughts in your head to believe, wondering if you're going crazy, trying anything you can just to survive each day. You haven't been able to identify yourself in this mess, make the decisions you want to make, and be the person you want to be.

So, it's time to forgive yourself for all the stuff you've been feeling bad about. Why not give it a try right now? Really do it. Tell yourself you've never had to be perfect. You're just one small person on this planet. And you happen to have a very debilitating mental health issue. Realize that you've always done the best you could do for that moment in time. And sometimes, when OCD has been at its strongest, the best you were able to do was to simply give in. And that's okay.

As you continue on your journey, your annoying travel companion OCD at your side but getting quieter with time, realize that you will fall into the OCD trap again, many times to come. And just as you're forgiving yourself for the past, promise yourself that you'll stop beating yourself up when it happens again. Your OCD companion is stubborn and convincing and will continue to make you do things you don't want to do. But if you can feel a little bit less guilty and ashamed when you faulter, this is going to make this process of regaining control of your life that much easier.

But This Is Not a Get Out of Jail Free Card

Repeat after me. "It is not my fault that I have OCD and have been doing all of these really unhelpful things for so many years." Now repeat this as well: "Now that I understand how my OCD works, it's also my responsibility to work on it." That's right. It's your responsibility to yourself, to the people you care about, and maybe even to the world to take back control of your life. And to show everyone what you have to offer. It's up to you to identify the person you want to be and the decisions you want to make. That is what this journey through life is all about. And hopefully you'll be traveling a little lighter now that you've dropped some of the baggage.

With that said, Bon Voyage. You've got this. You've always had this. Enjoy your travels and may you find the places in life that fill your life with meaning and joy, wherever they may be. You deserve it.

Reading List

Aardema, Frederick, & O'Connor, Kieron. *Clinician's Handbook for Obsessive Compulsive Disorder: Inference-Based Therapy*. Wiley-Blackwell, 2011

Foa, Edna B., Yadin, Elna, & Lichner, Tracey K. *Exposure and Response (Ritual) Prevention for Obsessive Compulsive Disorder*. Oxford University Press, 2012.

Grayson, Jonathan. *Freedom from Obsessive-Compulsive Disorder*. Penguin, 2014.

Harris, Russ. *The Happiness Trap: How to Stop Struggling and Start Living*. Trumpeter, 2008.

Hayes, Steven C. *A Liberated Mind: How to Pivot Toward What Matters*. Avery, 2020.

Hershfield, Jon, and Tom Corboy. *The Mindfulness Workbook for OCD*. New Harbinger Publications, 2020.

Huebner, Dawn. *What to Do When Your Brain Gets Stuck*. Magination Press, 2007.

March, John S. *Talking Back to OCD*. Guilford Press, 2006.

Polk, Kevin L., Schoendorff, Benjamin, Webster, Mark, & Olaz, Fabian O., *The Essential Guide to the ACT Matrix*. New Harbinger Publications, 2016.

Wagner, Aureen Pinto. *What to Do When Your Child Has Obsessive-Compulsive Disorder*. Lighthouse Press Inc, 2002.

Wells, Adrian. *Metacognitive Therapy for Anxiety and Depression*. The Guilford Press, 2011

Wilson, Reid. *Stopping the Noise in Your Head*. Simon and Schuster, 2016.

Acknowledgements

There are so many people who have made this book possible. Thank you to all of my colleagues at The Center for OCD and Anxiety in Pittsburgh, PA for helping me to always learn and grow as a clinician. Thank you to Amanda Meredith, my business partner and friend, for your energy in this field, and for your feedback on the manuscript. Thank you to my colleague and friend, Lisa Glessner, LCSW, for your careful edits. And thank you to my wife, for not only providing me with invaluable feedback as I wrote, but for never complaining about your sleep-deprived partner who was attached to his laptop during the writing of this book.

Lastly, thank you to my clients. It is a privilege to be trusted as a guide and support in your lives. You have taught me so much, more than anyone else, about this complex, often difficult, and always interesting, mental health issue we call OCD. May you continue to find peace and success in your travels.

About the Author

Michael Parker, LCSW

Michael is Co-Director of The Center for OCD and Anxiety in Pittsburgh, PA. He specializes in the treatment of Obsessive-Compulsive Disorder and other anxiety-related issues, blending both Exposure and Response Prevention (ERP) and Acceptance and Commitment Therapy (ACT) strategies. As a blogger, trainer, and therapist, he enjoys sharing his passion for these proven treatment methods with both those living with OCD as well as other mental health professionals.

His own travels have taken him everywhere from the small-town Pennsylvania of his youth to the sleepless energy of New York City to the epic beauty of the Pacific Northwest. He has found a home in a certain reinvented steel city in Western Pennsylvania and spends his free time exploring Pittsburgh and its surroundings with his wife and two sons. You can follow him through his blog at: pittsburghocdtreatment.com.

Made in United States
Troutdale, OR
06/07/2024

20382150R00139